1925 -
8ª

CAN YOU IMAGINE

by
Kelly K Owens

authorHOUSE®

AuthorHouse™
1663 Liberty Drive, Suite 200
Bloomington, IN 47403
www.authorhouse.com
Phone: 1-800-839-8640

First published by AuthorHouse   6/4/2008

ISBN: 978-1-4343-6700-6 (sc)
ISBN: 978-1-4343-7709-8 (hc)

Printed in the United States of America
Bloomington, Indiana

This book is printed on acid-free paper.

Table of Contents

Special Thanks

I would like to extend special thanks to my mom
and immediate family for their love and support.

I want to thank the following people for helping me with this
book: Deegon Wolf for listening to me and helping me find the
lost words and telling me I need to put them on paper. If it wasn't
for you, I would have just been speaking and not writing. And to
Melissa Todd for typing, so my words could finally be read and
also for inspiring me to add more depth to my words.

I would love to extend a special thanks to Dawn Alys
Capito for seeing a side of me that most people don't see and
for understanding the way I speak. Insuring my words were
portrayed to the reader, while maintaining the integrity of my
thoughts. Also, Kimberly LeMieux and Dahlila Martin for doing
whatever it took to proof-read this before it's final release.

These words come straight from my heart...

Last but certainly not least, Catrina Nelson for putting up with
me during my emotional moments, thinking about the past and
the present, and how I want life to be. As well as understanding
even when I didn't understand. Thanks for being that shoulder
and my rock.

You are all appreciated.

I promise you, we are going to change the world.

K. Owens

To purchase this book visit:

www.canyouimaginebook.com

canyouimaginebook@yahoo.com

Introduction

I am thankful you have chosen to read my thoughts so let's change the world together. Everyone is faced with different challenges. I have written about the darkness I faced almost losing my life at the age of 9. Growing up without a dad, we were not fortunate to have many things but the one thing we had was love. For some reason it seemed like we had it all. Growing up throughout the shadows, searching for some kind of light, and now for some reason I can appreciate life just a little bit more.

Take a long stem flower, give it to someone for no reason and at the same time you're finding the flower that grows within you. I can respect the long stem of a flower because of the strength it bears in order for it to grow so tall. Sometimes I wear my hat a little below my eyes just to be at peace and I get lost in a daze from the softness of the flower wondering what it is trying to tell the world... So I close my eyes to hear the soft whisper through the leaves. I am at one with the flower that grows within me.

This book is about my family I grew up with and the ones I have met along the way. I am fortunate to live in a neighborhood that seems like a fairytale. There is so much love. I live for the kid in me and the kids that I see. I embrace the future knowing what they are about to face. I know their future is bright because their parents are my friends and my brothers and sisters. Here is a glimpse of my celebrities. From the youngest to the oldest, I learn something new each day.

The purpose of this book is to bring to the surface lost words that have not been spoken and face what is vulnerable so we can strengthen who we are to have a better tomorrow. When you find yourself lost in words, trying to explain how you feel, flip through and find the page that represents you. Give it as a gift and say "this is how I feel"…

"Can You Imagine?" is written so you can close your eyes, open it to any page and find what reminds you of yourself or someone you know. Let your heart guide you to your page. I promise you will be amazed.

Here is my flower to you.

By

Kelly Owens

Blueprint

Write from your soul, not from your pen.
Your pen is only a tool to explain what you have within.
Let your heart guide you through the lines as if it's your veins.
Let's write for change!
Humble your soul with glory, embrace
that pen so you can tell your story.
Drop to your knees and ask the heavens for the strength
and knowledge for just a simple word that can be heard
throughout the valley.
The ink from the pen is not worthy of the story
that needs to be told.
This needs to be written in stone.
Heavenly Father, give me the pen
so I can write to all the women and men,
giving them the blueprint to get in.
Giving them the reasons why they were forgiven.
This story has been written in blood because we can feel it
through our veins.
Your map to heaven is within.
Can you see it? Can you feel it?
Can you feel your hands picking up a cup just for a drink?
Your eyes processing it.
Your reaching fingers grip for a sip.
Feeling that cup against your lips.
Isn't it amazing how your body works together without thinking?
Your heart works alone in the dark.
Your flesh is the true test being washed and clean,
dressed up to look the best...
Your journey is to get to heaven; look within

just how everything works together.
That's the way we should work on the outside.
Follow the blueprint of the blood within your veins.
Then you'll see the importance of change...
so therefore my life is not about a pen.
My story will be written through the changes of life.
The pain of understanding.
The will to get up and let my actions write again.
Life is not just life. Life is having life to receive life after life.
So you live twice being born again and forgiven for your sins.
Receiving the key to get in.

By

K. Owens

The Beginning of Time

In the most beautiful garden you could ever imagine there are grapevines everywhere. Tomatoes, cucumbers and plums as far as the eye can see. So many fruits and vegetables it would take your breath away. Collard greens so big, as if they had wings that fell from heaven. In the midst of all this tasteful beauty, there stand two with the duty to form the land. One man and one woman faced with obedience to the cause. Faced with the balance of change, being in love, and the passion that guides them to be with each other. They are faced with the change that can change life forever.

In the midst of this beauty there is a tree that stands as if it is reaching to heaven. It is covered with the most beautiful fruit. It is as if it demands attention from the world. It is as if you can taste it just by sight. Walking away seems impossible. Just below, there is every fruit you can imagine and every vegetable that your heart desires. The passion that guides you throughout your garden of life is within your reach. Being able to hold hands and finding the amazing grace within each other.

Understanding when the season is right, what to pick, planning for tomorrow and not being selfish for today. Everything must be thoughtfully considered to preserve your garden for the next season. Each footstep carefully planted in between the fruit. Every intruding weed must be cast away. Finding love within each other while understanding there is no lust and no rush for the beauty of the colors before you. It is understanding the knowledge of what it takes to be together as one, to take a step forward to preserve life for life after life for the ones to follow. Instead of picking from the tree, they chose the shade of the tree to sit under to share an orange. They are thankful for what has been given to thee… Take a blind eye to what satisfies you for today. Don't let the beauty of the forbidden lead you off your path.

From the beginning of time, everyone can make a change.

Let's make a change.

By K. Owens

First Day of School

The thoughts of a parent about their child's first day of school. Each summer they've done so much, and when I think about it, we could've done more. We've done so little. So much work to be done, having to be in three or four different places at the same time. Cleaning up this, cleaning up that. Trying to figure it all out because there is so much that needs to be done. Each night something from the day at hand carries over to the next day. School is coming up soon. Just give me a little room to catch up. No matter how many words I find to say how I feel, there still are not enough words for it to become real. I can't wait for school to start.

The day is here and now I'm starting to fear it. I'm fighting back the tears because I don't want them to go. For the past five weeks, I'm thinking that when school starts I can catch up, but now I do everything to keep them home just to be a little behind. It seems as if my child is stronger than I am at this moment because even if they cry at the top of their lungs not wanting to go, I'm crying harder than that. I cried the day before and all the way home. If they are happy because they want to go, I'm a little sad because they do. Why would they want to leave me? That's the selfishness that I'm fighting within my own little box that I'm dealing with.

Today is the longest day. A football or a little slipper laying on the floor…just the sight makes me cry. Five minutes have passed and I'm thinking that they should be home soon, but they just got there. What can I do with the time that I have when I was so behind and now I can't find anything to do when there is so much to be done? I need to get busy. I could pick up the phone and call somebody, put away some shoes, tuck the toys in the toy box.

I find myself in the kitchen cooking for not just me and then realizing that it is, just me and there are tears running down my face. How can I face the day when I looked forward to this day? Now I wish that this day would go away because I miss my child.

It seems as if the hands on the clock are not moving fast enough. I want to check the batteries to see if something is wrong, so I check my watch. I see that they're both the same. What are the odds that they are both slow, yet somehow I still doubt it. I pick up the phone to call a friend and they confirm their time is the same as mine. The first day of school when I was so behind and needed so much time to catch up. I would rather be wiping up ketchup from the counter from the fries that they've eaten. I can't wait. I can't wait. I can't wait but I have to wait. I find things to keep me busy even though I'm folding a shirt, it's taking me five minutes to fold it. I don't like the way it looks so I fold it again. When it is time for my child to come home, I feel like I'm the kid. I'm so happy. Now I'm faced with the second day of school and I will try to be strong.

First Day of School,
K. Owens

Hearts

I think you're an angel with a box of hearts to give to everyone. Your heart has to be pure so those you come in contact with can receive it in such a graceful way. And if your not, they wouldn't understand the blessing that was given to them because the form of your gift would change. Just when you get angry the sun shines brighter than it ever has before and it melts the purpose that you're giving everyone. The people who are waiting to receive it start to keep score. They start fighting amongst each other because of the form of the chocolate that was given to them... they have no clue what it was.

If you stay humble and accept the gift that God has given to you...what you're giving to them will be in the way that he has delivered it. Then and only then there will be no confusion between his kids. They have answers to his prayers because they have a symbol and something to believe in. You have a purpose so pay attention to how your sun shines because your anger and your happiness make a difference in others. Your purpose is to get people to heaven. Don't get angry along the way to melt the blessing that you're supposed to serve throughout the valley. Don't leave the people that you know and love confused trying to put it together and coming up with an excuse of why they can't make it.

Believe in yourself. Hold back the rays and give them a sunny day and show them the way. Keep the coolness within your heart so your message can be seen and heard. See the footsteps to heaven and be a light. A whole bunch of people running like it's a herd. Prepare yourself for what is to come because you are real and you have what it takes.

Believe in yourself.

Your life is not just about you; it's about others.

K. Owens

Do you love me?

Do you love me?

I am only asking because I just want
to hear it from you without a word spoken.

When I am around you nothing exists but what is present in my
mind is that moment existing with you.

So I am asking *do you love me?*

Does your love take you places even
when we are just standing still?

Because I am just wondering if
what I am feeling is beyond life because

I can't see having life without you.

At those little moments when we are not around each other

I feel like something is missing.

My love for you is so real it is intangible. It is not of this world.

I have never noticed the moon the way I do now.
Every little thing matters.

It is just because.

I am asking you *do you love me* the way I love you?

My love sets me free from all the challenges
I have ever faced, because

I don't have to do it alone.

I fell in love with my best friend.

Our friendship is better than any ship
that has ever sailed the ocean and

our love is the passion that guides us throughout the sea.

I adore the love we share.

Our love is sharing the same dream.

Even when they are different they are still the same

because we can both look at something
and have the same thought

but we are doing it in a different way.

It is just like our feet; there are a left and a right.
A left shoe on a right foot

it just doesn't seem right.

I love you because you let me be right,
when I am right, putting my strong foot forward as a man

and you standing by my side, step by step as a perfect team.

Your strength is just as equal, but in a different way.

Your soft voice can humble the giant in me.

You are my rock.

The essence of you takes control of me.

I know without you saying a word, I can sense it even when you are sleeping.

I feel like I can fly with a humble heart, with no wings because of the spirit that guides us that we've surrendered to.

Opening up our souls to take flight from the wind of heaven and being anointed from the breath of Christ to be worthy to take flight to be born again.

You do love me.

By K. Owens

Black or White
with Gray in Between

Relationships can be so hard because some people can be black or white or they can be in the gray areas, and it is all about their attitude. Black meaning for it, white meaning against it, and gray is indecisive; struggling to make a decision. How can we find someone who completes us because you can be white or against and they can be black or for it. Can you find a gray area in between to find out a little bit more about each other? Sometimes being in the gray gives you more time to analyze for it or against it. I was talking to a friend about a friend and they say what they like about that person is the confidence. It is either black or white with them. They always know where they stand. Sometimes that is not good because the anticipation of a decision that needs to be made is missed. My friend that is talking about a friend is gray.

It takes just a little time to make a decision and even then she still has doubts. But at least it was a decision that was well thought through. And in her own way she loves the black and white because it helps her find herself and in return he is getting to know her in the gray areas and he is finding more time to get to know himself, sharing thoughts, going for walks, planning trips. These things are well thought of between two people who are so different but so the same. So I guess in reality it doesn't matter what color you are as long as quick decisions are well-thought-out decisions that benefit you both.

Having the will to compromise.

What color are you?

By,
K. Owens

Stealing

Stealing you from yourself.
Caught up in the way the world is today.
Kids, drama, happiness, church, neighbors.
Brothers, sisters, and sickness and health.
Finding yourself worrying about everyone else,
and finding a way out just to find you.
Finding it would be not having to think about anything
but being blessed just to be.
Kids are raised; bills are paid, wondering where the next step
begins.
I can jump on a flight and visit any of my friends or all of my kids.
This is life.
This is life how I see it.
It's funny, going your whole life worrying so much
and working so hard and you forget so many little things,
and you miss a lot of the big things.
Working just to make ends meet.
Just so all the kids can have shoes on their feet.
Sisters and brothers standing between so we all get along.
Now being on your own and retired, stealing myself away from
the world ...
is the greatest feeling of all.
Now the world doesn't control me.
The control is the control within Christ.
So I feel young again.
I wake up in the morning and I want to run again.
I walk outside getting ready to run and realize I'm not that
young.
So you smile and shake your shoulder,
because there's nothing wrong with being older.
Stealing moments from time to time realizing you are aging like
fine wine.

Your smile is still the same; your heart is even bigger.
Your spirit soars like it's never soared before.
Your grace shows on your face.
Humbled from the trouble of the past with so much glory.
Slow, peaceful footsteps will be the true story.
Being happy for the time to come and embracing the moments of the past.

Thank you, Heavenly Father, for giving me the moments to steal time —
where I can reminisce about my kids when they were kids —and now they have husbands and wives
and they have their own family and it's not just their lives.
Trying to figure out where I fit in.
I know if I knock on the door, every one will let me in.
I know that. I feel that love.
I know that love because I taught that love
and I received that love from the ones who gave me that love.
Your mom, your dad...the love goes on.
So I'm fitting in and I'm sitting in amongst all my friends.
God has been good to us.

There's no rush about anything.
Enjoying everything at your own pace.

All the good things in life are the only things
that you want to focus on.
Because you've seen it all and overcome it all.
Thank you, Heavenly Father, for giving it all.

Stealing

K. Owens

Alcohol

Alcohol is a reality that is not a reality.

An illusion within itself to be lost.

Nothing is what it seems, judgment is impaired, and illusion is

not to be shared.

I will not put a thief in my mouth to steal my brains.

K. Owens

Is the Grass Greener on the Other Side?

I feel like a fish swimming on the bottom of the ocean amongst all the seaweed trying to find something to eat. Lost and alone so far from home but I can't help wonder about the view that is above. There is a sun shining and then it becomes a moon. Seeing the light, the way it reflects off each wave, it seems as if I forget who I am and where I am. With hopes that this place could be a better place and then one day the day comes. I swim as fast as I can just to get to the top because I'm so tired of swimming on the bottom. So focused on the view that is above even though it is blurry and it seems so beautiful. I forget about the surroundings that are around me. Finding everything wrong with where I am. Swimming as fast as I can go to where I want to be. By the time I get to the top I jump as high as I can to get to the light.

For the first time in my life I realize this place is not for me. I didn't know that you had to breathe air and you had to walk on land. For a slight moment, I saw it clearly. I couldn't wait to fall back in. I thought the shadows I saw flying above were so beautiful and now I realize those shadows are birds that feed off confused fish like me. Praying and hoping my weight will pull me down quickly before I'm seen.

Instantly my heart changes. I want to make the best of where I'm supposed to be. Gravity is not pulling me down fast enough. Taking every moment to see as much as I can see. At the same moment being confused because I can't breathe. I didn't know anything about the air. I didn't know about walking on land. The only thing that I thought I knew was that this was a beautiful picture and this is where I should be. Now I realize the grass could be greener on the other side but my life would be so much better living within my means.

Is the grass greener on the other side?

By,
K. Owens

I Believe I Can Fly

I have this vision. I am flying and all I can see is the ocean below. I look to the side and all I see are feathers all over my thighs and all over my arms and I realize I have wings. I fly as high as I can go. The further up I go, the more afraid I am. Gliding, following everyone who looks just like me, finding my place in that line. When I look behind, I'm not the only one.

All of a sudden, the line starts to glide down towards the ocean. It's hard keeping up. I feel so comfortable being me. Being free. Seeing everything that there is to see. Gliding over the ocean. Each swipe of my wing takes me a little higher. Each extension of my wing, with little ease I can feel the breeze.

The closer I get I see fish jumping out as if the water is boiling hot. There are so many waves, I can't count them. There are so many. Everyone is choosing their own spot to catch a fish just so they don't have to dive in. For an instant I realize keeping my belly full is easy. It's with no effort because the food is jumping up as if they want to see me. I can't eat any more because now it's hard for me to fly. My wings are getting tired. Just a little lost because I was having so much fun; I burnt up so much energy.

Looking for a place to land just so I can rest my wings. There's no land in sight. Flying as high as I can get and realizing I can't get any higher. Hoping I'm high enough so I can glide my way in. Even then, that seems as if it isn't enough. It seems as if I am not high enough because the ocean is coming up to the sky quicker than I can fly. It seems as if it's meeting me halfway. For the first time, I am aware that I have to preserve my energy, but it seems like it's too late. I close my eyes because for some reason I feel like giving up. Right before I'm plunged in facing the fact that it is over, I hear a voice. It is a fish that jumped out of the water trying to fly just like me. He is screaming at the top of his lungs. If my memory serves me right, that fish said to me, "It is worth the fight." I could make it. I could do this. I believe. For the first time in my life now I believe.

All of a sudden, I got a burst of strength and then everything went dark. Then instantly there was light. I opened my eyes and I see are people staring down at me. Beyond them there are birds hovering above. I looked over to shake the water off my wings. To my surprise, I see an arm with sand all over it leading to a hand that belongs to me. My heart filled up with joy and I started laughing.

Someone asked, "Why are you laughing? You almost just drowned." I just shook my head and said, "You wouldn't believe me if I told you but just be happy being you because life is worth fighting for."

I believe.

By,
K. Owens

Stay Young Forever

Crawling, wobbling when you walk, holding onto something just so you can stand. Slurring your words because you don't know what words mean. Your taste buds are on a runaway roller coaster searching for something simple. Smiling when someone is smiling at you, trying to mimic his or her expressions. Laughing when everything is funny. Running because you can and each time you fall you find the will to stand.

Nothing can keep you down because everything you desire is out of your reach. It takes a little more than what you have, to get what you want, so you learn how to stand on your tip toes and climb on top of things that you are not suppose to. Searching for something to wear because you want it to represent how you feel. Now you are learning how to put on your own clothes and tie your shoes. Stepping up to the plate with confidence knowing you can hit a home run.

Looking in the mirror as an adult, searching for the kid in you. Facing your biggest critic and your best friend all in one. Stay young forever because nothing can stop your dreams. Your hardest times have come to pass and you have overcome it because you are still here. The kid is within you, so smile and you will see it. Your critic needn't exist because each time you fell, the kid in you picked you up at your weakest and most vulnerable age as you reached out for life and taught you to never give up. Now it is up to the adult in you to take a lesson from the kid in you.

Coming into this world you didn't know how to speak, but you learned. You had no idea how to crawl. Your body is digesting foreign foods. Your eyes are processing each millisecond of something they don't understand. Your brain is working overtime just to keep up. Somehow through the crawling, falling, and trying to run you find yourself chasing someone who has faced those same struggles.

Stay young forever.

By
K. Owens

Definition of Love

Everyone says I love you at some point in their lives while searching for the definition of what love means, not just how love feels but also where it comes from. The word love is used lightly and it can confuse you when it becomes real. So if you ever get lost, here are simple words you can say.

I humble my love that is in bedded in my soul that only beats through my heart.

My actions have no choice but to surrender to its definition. Being anointed by the very creation from the creator of love. Making a change and instead of just saying it, becoming it, and overlooking all doubt with no regrets.

I am thankful for such a gift.

Definition of Love

By

K. Owens

Where Do I Go?

Where do I go from here? I look back at yesterday when I was a teenager. Life had everything to offer. The gleam in my eyes was so different than it is now because I didn't understand the purpose of life. I am thankful that I do have life. Each year, a different tear is shed but I grow older and wiser. Gaining different thoughts and learning more about life from moment to moment. Accepting the things in life where I have to dig down and be stronger than I was yesterday to make a way for the things that I've done and the things that I am doing.

I say I do because I love you, accepting you as my wife and now my life begins. The missing puzzle for the things that I've searched for I realize that I didn't have to search far because God has granted me the wish that I didn't know I had. When I close my eyes every night it's a peaceful sleep because I have someone to sleep next to me. She shares my memories and the thoughts of the kids and the grand kids and I'm not alone.

I have to face life in a different way now because I'm getting older. I can't carry all my kids on my shoulder like I used to but I can carry them in my heart as if they weighed nothing. Each one I have a certain love for. Each one I have a certain drive for and in any given moment I would die for. So where do I go from here? Do I bow down to my knees and shed each tear that I want to shed? I realize that my body is not like it used to be. I could run and be free as a bird and now I'm just like a gentle giant. I'm a little slower but I'm graceful. My smile is still the same. My thoughts are heaven bound because I know my prayers are answered.

Heavenly Father, give me the strength to get past the sickness so I can stand up and chase my grandkids and sit amongst my kids. So I can show them that there is a light at the end of the tunnel. I can be the example that I've always been. I know my prayers are answered and I shall not fall because I live every moment to see my grandkids crawl and begin to stand and talk and choose their words and put sentences together…becoming women and men.

I'm looking into the future because sometimes I'm scared for today. Just a blood clot in my veins and I look outside and it's beginning to rain. Most of my pain is within my thoughts because I'm used to being so strong but I'm thankful for my wife because I'm not alone. I'm thankful for my kids because they give me reason to live. I'm thankful for my grandkids because they are my stepping-stones to give me the strength to get out of that seat and to help my smile be a little brighter. To help my grip on the steering wheel become a little tighter.

My love is pure. I am thankful for today but I pray for today for my sickness and what I am going through to be at ease so the kids can hear the jingle of my keys when I'm walking up to the door. I am thankful for that. I believe and I know I shall achieve. I will stand up. I know there's no rush. I want to run but I know I have to walk. I want to scream but I'll soften my voice and I'll just talk. I will hug every grandchild and every kid because I am thankful for every moment that I live. Where do I go from here?

Sometimes I'm confused but I have nothing to lose because I've always taken a chance. At my old age I finally realize I have to turn the page to see life in a different way. I'm thankful that I have the strength to turn that page. I'm thankful to see this age. I am thankful for my kids, my family, my wife, my life. I know Heavenly Father will give me the strength to live twice. I'm asking, where do I go from here?

I will feel a little stronger. I will be able to get up like I did weeks ago. Sometimes the things that I fear are only heard within a tear. Some of my thoughts are just thoughts because I don't speak of them because I'm too strong. Some of my desires…I'm just a little too tired but I know I can make it. Even at the times when I feel like I can't make it, God has given me the strength to fake it. Standing amongst my grandkids when I know I don't feel well. Looking in my wife's eyes and facing my kids. They give me strength. Now I know where I go from here.

So I'm thankful for today. I know there will be a tomorrow. I'm thankful for my breath because I am breathing. I'm thankful for my eyes because I can see. I'm thankful for my fingertips and my arms because they help me hug all the people that I love.

I'm thankful for the love that I receive from above because now I know where I go from here.

By

K. Owens

One Grain of Sand

One grain of sand is what we are all searching for. If that is what you are searching for in order for your soul to be saved and you are approaching the beach to find that one grain of sand that represents your life amongst all the others, would you be discouraged and say that it is not possible because by the way that it looks, it is impossible? So it seems.

The way the water meets the sand seems such a fine line because when it is wet it sticks together and when the grains are dry they stand single and they are gathered together as one. So where is your grain of sand, the one amongst trillions? Will you be so discouraged if there is no hope and drop to your knees and pray and say that it isn't possible? How will you know, because each grain of sand looks the same and because the sand that represents you can be on the bottom of the ocean; are you willing to swim for it?

Or did it just get blown from the beach caught up in the wind or should you make a stand and call those you do know. And search for one together and be willing to save just one grain even if you are not sure that it is yours. Live your life right and one day someone can feel the same way you feel and save yours. We are all connected in the lost and confused world because the impossible is possible through the power of prayer. So reach and grab at least one grain of sand if you are just searching for yours but if you are out to help save others, grab a handful.

If you reach down just to grab one I am quite sure there will be others that will be surrounding your fingertips because when your heart is right, people are drawn to you and they want to be part of that. So by grabbing one you save others, and if you take that stand and hold it up to the heavens in front of the moon you can still see the moon, but if you pull it closer to you, close to your eyes, so your soul can see it, you can see that one grain of sand can block out the moon. It gives you room to see that you can save others. So look on your fingertips and you won't see just one, you see the presence of others even if they are so small your eyes could barely see them. One day someone will be in the position to save yours if you haven't already saved it. Being humble and willing to reach to help others you became that one-grain of sand reaching out to help others.

When you see footsteps in the sand just remember you are not the only one who has been searching and saving lives in the process. Those who are caught in your fingertips have no footsteps, so the only footstep that will be seen is the one who's been searching and saving lives.

One Grain of Sand.

By K. Owens

Cup of Coffee

Life is like a cup of coffee.

If you throw it at me, it will get all over me.

I'm not responsible for my first response.

If you hand it to me, I just might be able to appreciate it.

In simple words, let's not argue, let's sit down and talk.

Kelly Owens

Fighter

You are a fighter.

You're used to fighting for everything you live for.

You just have to stop fighting against something

or someone you already have.

If the battle is won there's nothing to fight for

and you have the victory of the battle to live for!

So let's stop fighting each other because the battle
has already been won.

Kelly Owens

Love and Anger

If you can conquer anger at the peak of being angry and misunderstood,

and have the will to listen in order to fight for love, sometimes,

all you have to do is just listen.

There are two sides to every story.

So listen with intentions to understand and then they shall be heard.

Then and only then you both will be understood.

So let's not point fingers unless you point at yourself.

When there is no pointing, there is room for change.

Kelly Owens

Lead and Follow

Isn't it wonderful that you can be a leader and follower
and stand in the same shoes?
You can follow your heart and believe in yourself
and have faith to lead yourself to safety.

Lead and Follow

Kelly Owens

Money

I'm broke and all my bills are due but somehow I feel rich inside because it doesn't cost me money to just be me. I can't buy that new shirt or shoes that I always wanted but I'm happy for the ones I do have. So money will never change my spirit. I believe in Christ and he has given me a pot of gold. A pot full of smiles, laughter, grace, love, understanding, forgiveness, and the will not to judge.

Have you ever thought about how unclean money can be? It changes hands every day. It can turn love into hate and can have you doubt your faith. Money can get you in the door and surround you with fake friends and fake love. Heavenly Father, I'm asking you to give us the sight to see through. Money can be loneliness and hate. It can lie to you making you think that you are bigger than you are. Some people carry it in their wallet or in their shoes, socks, and pouch or in their pocket.

In many ways it just doesn't seem fair. Money has been used in so many wrong ways. Used for drugs and starving babies crying; people are dying. So many lives have changed for as little as pocket change.

Nickel, dime, quarter, dollar — is this the faith that we are supposed to follow? Not. I can't wait until the day that people can see you as a million-dollar smile and walk up to you and give you a hundred-thousand-dollar hug.

That's what I'm searching for, the world to have that true love.

To me that's priceless.

Money

Kelly Owens

Co-sign

In life sometimes we need someone to co-sign.
To vouch for your credit, for you as a person, and in this case it's about your character.
Friends are your most reliable source and it's because they know you best.

The beginning of a friendship can lead to the best relationship.
If you fall in love being friends it's because no one knows you better than your friend.
Being friends in the beginning means talking about past relationships and present times and being able to laugh about them.
Facing jealousy head on with the comfort of knowing there's nothing to be jealous about because you have each other.

Relationships can get confusing because what we need sometimes is not what we're getting.
We assume our minds can be read because we are in love. And love conquers all.
In reality, love can only conquer when your friendship co-signs for the history and the reason why you fell in love.

Friends talk; lovers assume.

Let's talk so our love can bloom.

Your friendship paved the way so love can exist.

By,
K. Owens

Condom

Most people think condoms should be to protect you. The reality is they are not 100 percent. I think the wrapping around the condom gives you a moment to think about what you are doing, whom you are doing, and why you are doing them. What lives can be changed in a simple moment.

It takes effort to open. It takes time to think about the process of someone holding it in their hand. Is there love in the mix? Has there been time to find out whom you are with? Have you been to the movies? Out to dance? Or have you had any type of romance? Have you held hands, spent time talking to one another; do you know each other's favorite color? If you do, why do you choose the color that you do? Condoms are meant for you to think about what you are doing before you are doing who you are doing. You can miss so much if you don't know the reason why you are in the position that you are, so soon.

There are so many things in life that can change your life in an instant. A cute smile, a deep voice, a soft hello can be the very voice where you are blind and someone tells you that you have something that you didn't know. Think about it: Safety, relationships, getting to know each other…are more important than just getting with each other. Your body language can say so much. Your fingertips can have such a rush. Reality is lust and can have you getting yourself checked out for something you can't get rid of. Losing yourself thinking that you're lost in love when you didn't know the person when you woke up this morning.

Love, lust: We all fuss over the rush of getting to know each other and jumping over the rainbow and not realizing the true colors within each other and the reason why you want to be together. There is too much to lose. There are so many things that can be chosen from day to day to see if you can make a way to have a better day for tomorrow. We're leaving after the journey of saying hi and hello and what's your name? There should be no shame in saying let's wait, let's be friends, let's see where this takes us. If one day we become more and we can see more within each other than just the lust and the illusion of love, then and maybe then there should be a chance. We'll find romance when there is no physical, and within yourself you'll find someone that you never knew and that person will be new to you. So take a condom, have a condom at all times, and before the seal is broken, think about these words when it comes to the patience of getting to know each other so there is a purpose.

Condoms.

By K. Owens

We Just Met

We just met and I don't even know your last name. We just met and I have no idea about your fortune or if there is fame. There is something about you and I don't know what it is....

I was a little lost in words before I even spoke to you and the only thing that came out was hello. This is not about a rhythm or a rhyme because relationships and friendships are all about time. (Most people say timing).

My first question is what time is it? Do you have the time or can you find the time to find a friend within me? Or do I have the time or am I willing to make the time to find a friend in you? So I guess it is about timing. I took a moment to sit down and write something to ask you some questions. What day is your birthday? What is your favorite day of the week? What is your favorite holiday and why? What makes you laugh? What makes you chase something or someone when you know they are right for you? What makes you stay when you know it is wrong for you? I know it is hard to answer all of these questions at once so take your time and answer them one by one even if you are not answering them to me......

What are you doing right now? Are you sitting at the computer or holding your phone in your hand? Or do you have a cute smile on your face because this is all about you? (Made you smile) Are you the least bit interested in a new friendship? Because with a friend there is everything to gain but if I am not your friend we will never know the loss because until this moment we never even knew each other's names.

I can tell you what it sounds like when you laugh. I know the rhythm of your feet when you walk. I can pick out your silhouette from behind a curtain. I can close my eyes and pick your voice out of a thousand. I can walk away and laugh about your personality and have a grin on my face for five minutes after you've said goodbye because of your presence. Since we've met I look at my phone to see if there is a text but it wasn't from you. I checked my e-mail, I guess for a hint of a thought, I thought it would be you and then I realize that's my life before we met so everything is still the same because you have no idea what my e-mail is. I wonder what would change if we knew a little bit more about each other. I am not good at texting because it doesn't show my humor. Sometimes it is easier to read when the other person is too busy to talk (Understood) So what is your last name?? Because if nothing ever comes of this at least I know the first and I know your last…

We just met.

By K. Owens

The Greatest Love Song

The greatest song about love
can be the most beautiful thing that you've ever heard.

It can have such a sweet melody, but when true love is involved,
it is a great history of a memory of the way it was and the way
that it is.

There are two different ways to listen to a song:

You can listen to it and love it for something

that you're searching for
or humble yourself and enjoy the melody of the history —
of what you lived and are still living.

To me that's the greatest love song…
to have lived and still be living.

By K. Owens

Hi
=

Hi. How are you? How have you been and who are you? I have searched and it seems as if I've found. I found you. I've been through so much in my life and I felt as if I wanted to talk to you. I don't know your name, where you've been, or where you're headed. I just wanted to say hi because I miss what I don't miss but I miss it because I wish I knew you. I'm so confused at times because I don't know your name. I can feel your spirit because I'm writing to you. Within your own voice reading this you can hear your own voice sounding throughout your head. Even thought I can't hear it. I am thankful that you can feel it. Angels sent from heaven to find one another and we don't know where we're going to find each other but I found you. I just want you to know I love you. No matter where you've been or where you're going I love you for being interested enough to read my thoughts, my prayers, my pain, my desire, and what I want to share.

I know it's not much but I hope it's something that's just enough to touch your heart, your spirit, to change you just a little bit. To understand someone needs to hear you. I don't know you but I know you're someone special. You have to be for me to be sitting here writing this and for you to be where you are reading this. I had no idea it would be you.

Let's change the world. Are you okay with that? You know you are because you've felt this for so long. I felt your tears throughout the years. I've searched for people who have felt the way I feel. Now we are on the same page and we feel the same because you're reading this page. It means nothing without these black letters overlapping this white page to give a message. It's not about color because we're all sisters and brothers. I want to take this time to thank you for reading and listening to yourself reading these words from the beginning. Hearing it in your own voice inside your head. So hi, how are you?

By,
K. Owens

A Friend Just Told Me

A friend just told me that sometimes when I write,
I write about the things that are negative
and I'm not talking more about the positive.
Sometimes I talk about what I am going through
and I can't see a way to get through.
Sometimes it's sad but they reminded me that life is about being
happy.
With smiles on your faces, being able to sit in the bleachers and
watch the different races, not caring about the different colors of
peoples faces. The colors represent their different nationalities.

Knowing that this is reality.

Life is about that rainbow; the colors you see with your eyes
and the smile you have on your face.
It's about humming the Amazing Grace.
So I'm thankful for that voice to give me the choice of change
because it's not about being sad,
it's about the things that make you happy.
Sometimes when you talk about being sad,
it helps you get through the moments to find the happy ones.

So I'm saying let's be happy.
Let's talk about the positive.
Let's talk about when you slip and fall.
Let's talk about getting up and standing tall.
Let's talk about that twinkle in your eye.
Let's talk about the reasons that make you not want to cry.
Let's talk about the times where you want to be embraced
and you want to see that smile on someone's face.
Let's talk about when you just want to run down the street
and you just want to open your arms and your heart

because there is everything to be happy for.
Because you pray and you are thankful for breathing that fresh air.

So I'm saying I'm thankful for someone reminding us
that life is about being happy and being strong
and giving people the reason to live on.
Having what it takes so we can chase our faith,
not bow down for defeat.
So let's stand tall and have integrity.
Let's wipe the tears from our cheeks and let's shake our shoulders.
Let's call all our sisters and brothers and all our friends.
Let's let them know that it's time for all of us to work together
because heaven is coming close,
and it's time for us to get ourselves together so we are worthy.
Let's be positive.

A Friend Just Told Me

K. Owens

I Wonder What If?

What if we were friends?

What if we were more than friends?

What if there was life before life?

What if we knew each other then?

What if...life after life, what if?

I wonder if you will be my friend or more than.

I wonder if you hear my voice on the phone, will it be the voice to make you feel as if you don't want to be alone?

I wonder if we went for a walk, would you want to hold my hand

or just walk by my side?

I wonder if you felt the same way or would I feel the same?

Can you see me now or can you see me back then?

Or can you see us in life after life?

And if you can where would we be?

I have so much to say but the words have never been heard.

Would you want to know?

I wonder if I ask you a question, would you answer?

Do you want to know what the question is and why?

We can be, we will be, only what we see, what God has given to us.

So the answer will lie within, so let's see.

I wonder if at the end of this we will say to one another, what if? Wonder / What If?

My friend, my love, it's the love that we have for each other which gives us wings so we can fly together.
Or will it be a feather that has fallen from the wings of our journey
that we've flown together?
I wonder if someone walked on the feather that has fallen from us, would they feel the grace of heaven and the love forever and peace from the footsteps that can never be walked on.
Because love is something you fly on.
I wonder if they look down and not see the ground, would they not feel afraid.
Because their journey has just begun.
Peaceful footsteps that have fallen from heaven,
from two angels who have wondered, what if?

I Wonder What If?

By Kelly Owens

SIX PACK

ONE... Your strong will can be felt when you first step into a room. Your strong will, not to give up doing the best of the best so you can be the best.

TWO...Your physical is such an unfound treasure. It's like following the rainbow searching for a pot of gold. Realizing when you get to the end, your true treasure is within.

THREE...Your free spirit is like a feather caught in the wind. When the wind blows, no one will ever know the weight that you possess. The journey of a feather that has fallen from heaven from one of the two angels that wondered what if? Our spirit is the feather that is carrying on the legacy of two angels that fell in love. Peaceful footsteps reborn.

FOUR...The way you walk and possess the space you're in with a soft smile, a gentle laugh, and the will to listen at the peak of when you're misunderstood. You are a true feather.

FIVE...Your intelligence is in a world within itself.

SIX...Your drive to do what's right, looking into the future so you can make a way for today. Having goals so you and yours can become more complete. Keeping your heart right and being strong for others. Don't forget about yourself in the mix of taking care of others. Stay true to yourself and don't be afraid to express yourself. Here are six things about you. It's time to pack because your journey has just begun.

Six Pack
K. Owens

Dream

My dream is a dream; at least that's what it seems. I feel like I'm in a deep sleep, but at the same time I feel like I'm awake and standing on top of the world. I don't know if I want to wake up from this dream, because everything is like I see it in my dreams. If I'm awake I don't want to fall asleep because I'm living my dream.

My dream is to walk outside and all the kids are running and playing. I want to see all the people driving by waving at one another like we are sisters and brothers. The mountains have painted the perfect picture today. I can't believe what I'm seeing from my eyes. They are covered in snow, and when I squint my eyes I can see the little trees. The sun is slowly chasing the shadows from the deepest point of the mountains. Just below I can see homes that are surrounding the mountain like a pearl necklace because what I see is the snow slowly melting from the rooftops. I raise my hand to shield my eyes from the sun while the clouds are slowly hovering above. Now, that to me, is a dream and reality. So let's not take our dreams for granted. Notice the beauty of nature and life that co-exists and paints the most beautiful picture that you can ever dream of. You can live it!

So we pulled over, Deegan and I to the side of the street, because the mountains were a sight to see. We might be a little late to where we are headed but it was worth the wait. Now that's fate! Cars are passing us by with so many lives headed in every direction. I can't help to wonder if they see what we see or is it they are just too busy?

So let's pray:

Heavenly Father, we are sitting on the side of the street
pointing east, noticing everything that eyes can see.
Give us all that it takes to slow life down, just enough so there is
no rush.
Give us the strength to look in the cars next to us
and the homes that we pass and be humble with the spirit of
Christ
and know that we are one.
Help us understand that it's not our job to judge; it's our job to
love even when we don't understand.
Give us the will to face our own trials and tribulations
and only compare ourselves to who we were yesterday.
Give us the strength to ask for forgiveness for our sins so we can
make a better tomorrow.
Thank you for the grace, forgiveness, and the unconditional love.
In the Lord, Jesus Christ's name, Amen.

Let's not let life pass us by.

Let's dream our dreams and live our dreams so one day we can
have our wings.

Dream
Kelly Owens

Today

Today is a good day.
Smile from your heart and laugh from our soul.
Embrace all your moments that make you laugh.
Only think of those moments at the end of your day,
so therefore today is a good day.

By

K. Owens

Single Mother

One day I had to face life, life within me, and find a way to be an adult in order to set life free.

I never knew that life from me would take a big part of me.

I don't know the first steps to make, but if I stop, my family will not survive.

I find ways to make it and at times have to fake it.

Just to put dinner on the table for the first time in my life, Heavenly Father, give me strength so we can have life.

I've fallen asleep with dry tears on my face not knowing tomorrow what it is I have to face because I'm not alone.

My baby cries but he can never do any wrong.

For the first time I know what it feels like being alone when you're not alone.

I pray to the highest of heavens, why me? Why me?

I look at my baby's face and I can never say that I can give him away.

I just pray that today will be the day that all mothers can take a stand raising a child without a man.

I believe in Christ, and every time I hear that cry he doesn't cry alone.

I will be the best that I can be and I will give it all just to see that day for my baby to crawl.

Now I see for the first time that life is not about just me.

Heavenly Father, for whatever it is bless me and my child so we can give the world a reason for worth and a reason to live on.

Single Mother,

By
K. Owens

Baby's Mama

Sometimes we men people refer to our baby's mama and that means there is drama. Usually the drama is from what we created. When we first met her she had a name and there was no baby and there was no drama. Something changed in order for her to be called "my baby's mama".

We wonder why we fight from time to time to see our kid. We're confused because she won't let us see him. She's confused because we don't try to see him. We're upset because we want to see him when we want to see him and we don't understand why that's not okay with her. She's upset because we only want to see him on our terms. Weeks and months have passed and we want to see him when we want to see him.

Either way our baby's mama is because of the drama that we've created. It's not that she doesn't want us to see him. She just wants us to step up to the plate and be a full-time dad because there's no such thing as being a part-time dad. The only part-time dad that does exist is with people in our neighborhood or our friends and family. The men that come around are part-time dads because kids in some way look up to adults. A real dad is one who helped the seed. There's no way he could be a part-time dad to his own seed, but he could be a part-time dad to someone else's.

I guess the main thing is being a man and understanding why there is so much drama. It gets the drama started by running away. Looking at the phone sometimes and not calling because you don't know what to say. Playing basketball when your child is at home just beginning to crawl. Laughing and playing with your friends when your baby's mama is wondering when you're going to finally step up to the plate. So when you ran to make the call there was drama and rightfully so there should be. Your excuse was that you were confused and what you didn't realize was that when you're confused, she was confused, but she didn't run and if she did, she had your child in her arms. When you ran, you used your arms just to keep standing, to balance your weight. She faced sleepless nights staying up with your child. Now you're faced with the same and all you have are empty walls facing the biggest mistake of your life. How could you have been so blind?

You need to stop referring to her as "my baby's mama" if she's no longer "my" because she said goodbye. She is a mother not a mama because she's doing it. You have to step up to the plate and not be ashamed to call her by her own name and finally realized that buying shoes and buying clothes is not child support it is your responsibility as a parent.

Running away but coming back years later doesn't make it better because there's so much time lost. When someone is confused it doesn't mean the other person knows, just one person is in a position to have to try know even when they don't know. They have to show love and learn love and see love.

When you were running away from love you were running from your child, finding every reason to make it seem as if she was wrong. Picking up the phone and she had an attitude and it gave you another week to do what you needed to do. It's a sad case for a man that has to say "my baby's mama" because when a man says it in that way, we — they — have to think of why it's called my baby's mama drama. It's about the baby that we're neglecting, the drama because we are not there and the mama that is upset because of it. My means my mess that I've gotten myself into. When there's a life that just has a mom to look up to when a father is running trying to find how to be a father. You can't find it when you are running you can only find it when you are running towards that life. Even when you don't know, the fact of being there means more than walking away. Of course, it's not going to be the easiest road but it will be the best road that you've traveled. Someone who looks like you and who is a part of you — you can see their life as it's unfolding and find love for someone who is so young coming up when they don't know what the world has to offer.

You face yourself and your mistakes that you've made. You face the woman and say that you're sorry. Even if she accepts or if she doesn't accept, find that true friend that you had from the beginning so you can be there. Then it can have a happy ending so there's no baby's mama and there's no drama. There will be a baby that has a mama but no drama.

Let's get it together. Time is getting short.

No More Drama.

Best of Friends

By
K. Owens

My Past

I was always afraid of facing my past.

My past is okay because I ask for forgiveness.

Now I smile about the ups and downs

that I had to go through to get here.

Sometime I can't help but shed a tear.

My past is blurry because I can only see it through my tears.

By
K. Owens

Back in the Day

Back in the day all of the songs and music that we heard were more about love than lust. They were about loving someone and holding their hand. About a woman searching for a man and a man being the best gentleman he could ever be. Listening to the melody on the radio. Back in the day. It wasn't perfect but the most important part of music and what people had to say was more about survival and about understanding each other and about the essence of a person. The songs now are more about undressing someone. When we listen to the words that are being said, they are so graphic, and when you listen to the melody and the sounds of the beat it makes it sound so right when it's so wrong.

Let's go back, back in the day. Wouldn't you love to hear a song about walking in the park and holding hands? Two people who are nervous because they don't know what to say to one another but they know there is love. Holding hands with just trust. Whether it's following the moon they're gazing over the city or reflecting off the water hovering over the trees or a walk over the countryside. No words being said and not being misled by something that is too graphic. It's just about the moment when you're falling in love and there's nothing to say. It's just about the moment.

The years have passed and now that love seems as if it doesn't exist because our music is so graphic. It's to the point that if you really listen you have everything to lose and nothing to gain. If you gain something, the change will rearrange your life — not in a good way. It's all about this; it's all about that when it should be about rewinding time. Going back to where a man opens the door and the woman is pleased to be teased. A man is humble because he put a smile on someone else's face and it wasn't about anything graphic.

Back in the day. Someone could bake you a cake and make it themselves. Each ingredient is thought of even if it wasn't thought of from them alone. They had help from a mother or a sister or a father from afar yelling from the living room. It was about family. Nowadays it seems as if it's all about the bedroom when in reality there is no room for love; there's only room for lust.

Back in the day. I wish that we could erase the day that we live in so we could go back to the values. Where people sat down with a pen and a paper and wrote about feelings. They wrote words they didn't know how to say and they found a way of saying it even if they didn't speak it because the melody tickled their heart for the words they couldn't find. I want to hold hands like yesterday. I want to walk in the park like years before. I want someone to write a song with no lust. I would love for it to be about love and about how I feel when I see someone that I care for. That's what I'm searching for. For it to change, because if it doesn't change all we're going to have is change. People changing prescriptions for what they have. Changing clothes to see another. Changing attitudes just to fit in.

If you feel the way I feel, make a stand for what's real. Find a tape or an old record player and play some old tunes for that real love that you would love to see soon. It's not about a rhyme; it's not about what someone's driving. It's not about what someone has. It's about finding that love that we lost from the past. So let's go back. I love you and I hope you love me too. I would love to hold hands. I would love to run for no reason. I would love to love without a rhyme of a word to bring you closer. Just being able to find a word that is real within my heart so we can be closer. We can go fishing, cooking in the kitchen, and have a picnic on our front lawn. It's about the silent moments waiting with anticipation for the phone to ring, listening to each car as it passes by wondering if it's them. The perfect silent song in the midst of waiting for someone can be the most beautiful words ever heard if they can be put on paper or those feelings can be captured in a song.

Let's go back. Back in the day.

By,
K. Owens

Peaceful Sleep

It's been a hard day at work trying to take care of everybody
and make sure everything is done.
Trying to find some sleep to get things out of my mind.
Chasing it, tossing and turning, but when I do find it it's a deep
sleep.
Dreaming about the reflection off of the water
through the trees when there's no light behind.
Trying to find that deep sleep.
Tossing and turning just a little bit, not really awake but not
really asleep.
Dreaming of different dreams, half of them I can't remember
but I know it is a dream.
My body is tired; my mind is tired.
So this is what I've been searching for all day
is to hold this pillow the way that I'm holding it now.
Peaceful sleep.
My one chance to get away from the world and live in a world of
my own.
So I find peace when my eyes are closed.
My arms close to my head...two to three pillows.
As much as I can get to make me feel more comfortable
knowing that I have faced today and tomorrow it starts all over
again.

So I take advantage of it.

I think about the blessings that I've had throughout my day and
the people who are dear to me that I wanted to call today but I
didn't have time

so I called them in my sleep through my heart.

That helps me sleep, thinking of that love, that comfort.

That's peaceful to me. A silent prayer.

I'm just so thankful to be able to have a place to sleep.

And praying for the moment to wake up but at this point it's
about my peaceful sleep.

I want to think about nothing.

I want my mind to go blank, and for some reason there's
something always there.

Always there.

By the time I hear the alarm clock it's time to get up again...

to get dressed, brush my teeth, get something to eat.

I'm thankful for another day to start it all over again.

So I thank thee for my peaceful sleep.

Peaceful Sleep
K. Owens

Where Do We Go from Here?

Where do we go from here when our lives are so conditioned...
on work, bills, what to do, what not to do, and just trying to keep
food on the table?
There's so much that we miss.
We miss why our kids are feeling the way they feel.
We miss how come our nieces or our nephews are going through
what they're going through and they need someone to talk to.
A lot of times we miss our moms or dads, grandmas, grandpas,
sisters, brothers, friends.
When does it ever end?
Do we miss them because we never make time for them?
Because all our time is trying to find time for ourselves when we
are not working?
When is there going to be a change, and how do we change?
Do we talk to our kids more about how they are feeling rather
than their homework?
Or do we talk about their homework more
than why they are feeling the way they feel?
Or do we find the time to talk about both?

Somehow or another we all need to get to know one another...
our sisters, our brothers, our uncles, our aunties, and everyone
else.
Because we are losing so much just trying to find ourselves
and sometimes finding ourselves is finding it within someone else.
Because some of the things that we feared, we can deal with
better
when we are listening to their tears or they are listening to us.
So where does it start?
How does it start?

Work is crazy. Bills are due.

When do we find the time when life is about you? Us?

Some people have problems in their school and following the rules.

Some of us have problems in our work.

Can't wear a skirt; have to wear a suit or a tie.

I wonder why. Is it more about an image?

Is it more about how we look than how we feel?

Is it more about what's not real?

No matter what we are wearing we should always be caring and sharing.

That's life.

That's where we start.

We start with not trying to change people.

Being able to listen and if someone listens to us,

I guess that's where the change starts.

I don't know. You tell me.

How can we deal with our kids and our friends,

when they have so many questions about what we see on TV...

who stole a car, how many people got killed overseas,

who had this disease or that disease.

Where does it start?

Does it start by us trying to be more positive and keeping the dangers

from the ears that are so humble that are going to be leaders

of this country one day?

Do we shelter them from all of the problems in this world?

I don't know, but I know we need to shelter them from some things.

The things that they don't understand, they should not hear.

Only woman and man should be able to deal with that.

That's why it should be different.

If there's some bad news then it's not good news.

If it's bad news, we should have the option to choose who listens.

Because when someone does something across town
and you hear about it in your living room,
that seed is planted in the minds of the innocent.
Having kids be kids when they are all up in our biz.
Something has to change.
We need to protect them from the things that they don't need to know about
and teach them the things that are to come.
So when we hear about it we need to be the filter that filters
things to our kids so they can stay kids and learn how to be adults,
by us being adult enough to be adults.
Let's find that way.
Let's come together.
If you have an answer, tell somebody.

Let somebody know because every great grandpa or grandma
or mother, father sister, brother, cousin
has always been confused about something.
Two people can stand right next to each other and both be confused
but they both can have the answer if they just speak up and talk
and you realize; there it is.
We have an answer for our kids and for our family.
We found it.
Because Christ has it within you.

Every problem and everything that you deal with in life is within you to find.
So reach out to those that you care about.
Find out more about their lives.
Talk to them while they have their head down.
Ask the kids, why do you fight with him or her? Why?
Really ask WHY and find a solution.
If you don't have a solution, the solution is the fact

that you are there to be in the middle so that is change.
Let's turn the TV off a little more.
Some news comes on early, we can watch it later.
It always repeats itself.
Let's help our kids be kids.
Let adults be adults, because how can they be kids
when we're confused about being adults?
When they listen to the same things that we do?
So whether we have a suit, a tie, a skirt, or a dress, slacks, khakis,
blouse...
whatever it is, let's protect our kids.

But don't forget that you are a kid too because you are a child of
God.
So protect yourself. Some things are hard to listen to and deal
with
when you are carrying a burden of your own.
It's hard to be happy when you know there is so much pain in the
world.
Work on your circle and talk to the next circle and they'll work
on their circle.
Before you know it, it's a chain reaction.
We all link together and it's a perfect necklace around Christ's
neck.
A chain reaction.
It starts by one then two then three then four then five.
Then we can thank God that we are here and we are alive.
So let's make a change. You have the time.
Make the time so when it's your time,
somebody is there the same way that you were so it repeats itself.

Where do we go from here?

K. Owens

Raindrops

Searching for a word that can represent how I feel about you.
I am getting lost in thoughts and finding myself crossing over
into a fairytale,
just to find a way to show you and find a word to tell you.

The more I think about it the more confused I get
and all I can think about is a raindrop.
A raindrop can be the tear of love that is shed and it can be the
rain that is heard outside a window nurturing life that grows
right before us. My rain to you is each time you see a smile, it's a
raindrop.
When you receive a gift, it's a raindrop.
When you are thought of, it's a raindrop.
Put your hand on your chest and feel your heartbeat, it's a
raindrop.
Prepare yourself for the storm that is to come.

And if you hear the thunder rumbling it's just me getting lost in
words and being confused because I can't find the words to show
you so I give you raindrops.

I love you.

Raindrops.

By,
K. Owens

Blessings

Counting my blessings, where do I start?
Do I start by counting the beats in my heart
or the tears in my eyes?
I see my blessings right before me!
As my eyes are reading this paper, I'm blessed to be able to see.
I'm blessed to be able to hold this paper with one hand or two.
I can feel blood flowing through my veins
and know I will be protected when I'm walking out in the rain.

Can you feel your blessings?

Think about what you see right now. Think about how you feel.
Think about the people in your life that need so much!
Think about the people who love you.
Think about the roof that's over your head.
Think about the shoes and socks that you have on your feet.
If you don't have any then the blessings alone, are your feet.
Are you starting to see and starting to feel why you are blessed?
What do you hear in the background while you're reading this?
You're blessed to have ears.
Believe in your blessings and they will help you face your fears!
Now your tears will be tears of joy, knowing that you are alive.

Are you standing or are you sitting?
I guess it doesn't matter; you're blessed.
Think about all of the good things that happened throughout
your day and at the end of each day.

Therefore, there are no bad days.
We are blessed to hear the alarm clock, even though there are
others who have passed on.
You're blessed to get out of that bed
and by the time you're washing our face,
you should be humming the Amazing Grace.
So I guess it's not about counting your blessings,
because we could never keep score.

I thank thee for the days that have passed and the days to come;
give me the strength to press on.

Let's be careful about the things that we speak!
Stay true to what is real and in
that case you shouldn't have to whisper.
Scream at the top of your lungs!
Because you have what it takes to read this
or to hear it being read.
Life is not about statistics; it's about what you make of it
and how much passion you have in reaching your goals.
You've spent three to five minutes reading this,
minutes you can't get back.
So now do you see how important every minute in your life is?
Every minute can be a closer step to heaven, so let's not waste it.
Put a smile on your face and let's go!
If I don't see you here I'll see you at the pearly gates…
And if you're a minute late, just believe in faith.

Blessings,
K. Owens

Thinking of You

Monday through Friday...

First day of the week I wake up
with a smile thinking of your laughter.

Tuesday was more of a fairytale chasing you
with nothing to lose
but everything to gain.

Wednesday is the day when I realize
that Monday and Tuesday
were just a dream.

Thursday sets in and I realize that you've only been in my
thoughts.

Friday tossing and turning chasing a dream
that is within a dream.

Just a little scared of reality for the risk of losing my dream.

Instantly I'm awake...first thing on my mind is to hear your voice,
stop by just because.

It doesn't matter to me if its reality or fantasy because

...Within this week you brought great joy to me.

Thinking of you

By
K. Owens

Stay at Home Moms

It's hard trying to find where to start and tell you how much you are appreciated. When I say how much you are appreciated, it means being in the position to stay at home with your kids. To show them the true values of your heart. Telling them what not to do and what can be done. Having the comfort of someone who is a part of you working hard so that dream is not a dream, it's a reality that some people dream of. At the same time understanding that each day the voices that you hear are of babies or of kids growing up.

As an adult every day you're talking to kids. Every day you have a grown adult coming home talking about grown-up things. Somehow you have to adjust. This goes out to you saying thank you for being the mom or the dad and for making it happen. When a mom or dad can stay in their home and hustle making it happen. Sometimes the world forgets about a full-time job that is at home. No matter how much you clean, the house still never stays clean. No matter what you do, at the end of the day, no matter how much time you have it's still never done. Throughout your day you're chasing your son or your daughter. You have someone who loves you who is chasing a dream in a paycheck to make sure no one else is raising their child. That's the greatest triangle that ever existed.

Two people understanding that there is a purpose and the purpose is for their kids and their family. One working hard for what it takes to keep it going and the other working hard for the same purpose. No one's job is really more important than the other, because your job is never done. Washing dishes is like a never-ending story. Getting up and facing work seems as if it's **your** only story, but you're happy to come home to hear the story that **you** are working so hard for. It will be a great story, just believe.

Stay at home mom, you are the greatest. You are one of the most envied persons that there is because you're one on one with your kids. When they come of age or if they're all still in school, no matter what, you still make them follow the rules. For the sole provider who's keeping a roof so there are no leaks when it rains, opening your heart and your arms — covering, so your family doesn't see the pain that you have to deal with every day just to make it happen.

Each person can say that their job is more important than the other, but we all know they're just the same. It takes both of you to make a change so a diaper or a pair of shoes can be bought. A little child being potty trained can be taught. A husband or a wife can be happy for these things when they come home and they can be happy because there is a home. Stay at home mom walking your kids around the block. Talking to the neighbors about some of the things or the same things that you talked about the day before.

Each day your kid is getting a little bigger. Your sunshine is getting a little brighter because he or she is a little fighter.

Blessings in every way that you can see it. Blessings in every way that you can feel it. Nothing can be taken for granted because you know what's real. Lying down on your pillow tonight, face to face, and you know that you're a team. To the sole provider; when you come home, understand that the person there has been talking to kids all day. We know your day has been long, but understand that it takes a little bit of time to adjust to talking to an adult. For the one who stays home, understand that he or she has been talking business all day and just needs a moment so they can enjoy the rest of the day. Find that happy moment and that balance between the two so the love between the two of you — your seed can see you as one. If there's something that needs to be discussed on an adult level, it's discussed behind closed doors. If you have to raise your voice just remember you have a choice to whisper. Because what you both are working hard for is for that whisper to not be heard.

The true love of the balance of you coming together creates the greatest seed. Stay at home, go to work, work together — you are appreciated.

Stay at Home Moms
K. Owens

My Secret

My secret is not having a secret.

Following your heart for what is to be and not to be.

So therefore there are no secrets.

Chase the times that you have

that make you feel complete at all costs.

By
K. Owens

Believe in Yourself

You can't be you unless you believe in yourself because no matter what life lies ahead, you have to believe in yourself in case you fall when there's no one there. You have to pull yourself through, so believe in you. The most important person in your life, is you. The most important person to believe in is the one who created you. Think about it. You have to tie your shoes. You have to feed yourself. You have to wash yourself and dress yourself and present yourself in a way that you want to be presented. Your life is about you not what people say it's about — you and the one who created you. You couldn't do the things you do if it wasn't for the one who created you. Before the time you had time to find the time to be somebody. Somebody had to be somebody to make sure you are somebody. Keep that in mind.

Don't be confused because there is life after life. There was life before you had life, so believe. Take a stand. Don't be afraid to be yourself. Silence your ears amongst your peers so you don't make choices to please them. Humble your heart and believe in what you want to achieve within life. Then you can feel that realness within you and you can be someone to follow. Either a kid or an adult will say, "I want to be like him or her."

So believe in yourself and believe in your creation. Life is not about an apple tree, but in the same sense it is about an apple, and a tree, and our creation. What's right, what's wrong? Believe in yourself and don't change your belief just because you like the melody of a certain song. Listen to the words and what they mean because sometimes a melody can have you searching for something that has never been seen or something that is not right or something that someone else believes in. When it's your day to face the day and the end of your days…you have to face the decisions that you made. Think about standing in front of the apple tree. What is your decision? Will you bite or will you choose what's right? Life has been given to you so it's up to you to do something about it. Trust and believe with the creation of your heartbeat and the blood that is flowing through your veins. Don't be ashamed of slipping and falling. Just be the man or the woman that has crawled for the experience to stand again so you don't make the same mistakes.

Believe in yourself.

If you don't believe in anyone else, believe in the creation of all of us.

The Creation.

K. Owens

Hold Your Tongue

The perfect person is someone
who loves everything and everybody
and has the strength to move mountains
and to see in your heart
how you feel at all times.

The perfect person can change the weather
with a blink of an eye
and be able to see the world
and hold the world in the palm of a hand.

The perfect person was crucified and still forgave us for our sins.
If you can walk across water or walk through the snow
and leave no prints or can part the seas...

If you can see yourself doing these things,
then and only then do you have the right to judge me.

Jesus is the one that went to the river and walked about,
so don't talk about, unless you can go to a river
and you can walk about
and then, you can talk about.

Hold Your Tongue

By
Kelly Owens

I Don't Wanna

Tossing and turning, the light coming through the blinds of the window. I know it's time to get up to go to work. I don't wanna go to work today. I didn't get enough sleep. So many things on my mind that I couldn't put behind. I know I have to go. Rolling out of bed slowly, body so tired, but I have to see myself in the mirror so that I can see clearer to find a way to get to work today. I don't wanna. I don't wanna deal with the phone calls or walk in the office and find paper all over the place. Some filed right, some filed wrong. I don't wanna deal with that today. I want to disguise my voice a little bit to sound like I'm sick just to call in. I know I have to go. I have to get up, be strong.

I can do it. I know I can. I've done it over and over before, I've just got to let my feet touch the floor. Feel the carpet, feel something beneath my feet to stand up. To see that clearer in the mirror. Brushing my teeth trying to wake up, slowly getting strength. Seeing things that remind me of life that I didn't put there. Now I'm getting strength about all those things that I care about...my family. For some reason, I feel a little joy. Not much but just a little bit. Is this what I have to go through every morning, just to find my way to get a way to face the day? I'm reaching for it.

I thank God that I'm in a position to have life, so my smile is getting a little bigger. Looking for clothes. Something to put on my body to represent how I feel today. If it were how I felt ten minutes ago, I would put on some pajamas and grab a pillow, get in the car and drive to work. But I'm feeling better because I can see the love; I've received the love. And I'm praying to the heavens above for the strength to get through this. So I think about all of my family and kids and friends. Then I realize my clothes that I have are fitting so nice. I look okay. This is my day.

I'm going to make a way for the loved ones so they have a reason to say that they want to get up and face the day. I can be an example. I'm going to do it; I'm on my way.

Walk out and start the car...look in the mirror and say to myself — you know who you are. You are blessed because you passed the test so you are here. So driving, seeing other lives and other people out on the street going to work and some on the way home, I find myself glancing as the cars pass by. Just wondering if they are on the way to or from. But it's okay because I'm working towards my loved ones. So I find myself just going a little above the speed because it's time for me to get there because I'm going to make it and I'm going to do it.

Thank you; Lord, for giving me the vision and the strength to push through it.

I don't Wanna
K. Owens

I Miss You

I miss you because all day today, all I could think about was you.
It seems that life has changed so much over the years,
and it's hard to see things the way it really are through all the
tears.
Every challenge of life it seems as if there's a change within us,
to make us tougher for tomorrow.
I don't know why that is.
I pray for better days and better ways...
to find ways to get through the day.
I miss you.

I'm missing just cooking eggs in the kitchen.
I'm missing riding that bike up and down the street
and every face that I saw wasn't a stranger.
I miss those days.
I miss you.

I miss the times working out,
doing everything that can be done to stay in shape.
That's why I miss you.

You motivated me.
It wasn't anything that you did special,
you motivated me by just being you.
Young, so many ideas, so many dreams...
and everything you were going to accomplish no matter what.

I can sit here and cry a thousand tears,
because the hardest thing for me to do is face my fears.
I fear tomorrow, I fear next week because it's hard...
just trying to just be me all the time.
I miss you.

You were my best friend and I don't know where things came to
an end...
but you were my best friend.
No matter what I needed, you were always there.
No matter what I had or you had, we were willing to share.
And if there was anyone in this world,
I knew it would be you because you cared.
You helped me put my shoes on, my socks, all my clothes.
You helped me pass tests.
You helped me do it all.
You helped me crawl and try to stand
to be somebody in this world...
and I'm saying I miss you.

So I'm trying to find ways to get you back...
so I can be who I'm supposed to be.
Because there is something within you that I have to find,
in order for me to be free.
I'm standing looking in the mirror..
Looking at you and you look just like me.
Tell me what you see within me that will set me free.

Sometimes in life we all get lost; it's all about finding ourselves.
Who we used to be and how we used to be.
Sometimes we lose it as we're growing up.
Let's remind ourselves how to find ourselves.

I Miss You

By

K. Owens

Copying

In life sometimes we get upset when someone copies us. You buy a purse and your friend buys one just like you. You buy a pair of shoes and those are the same shoes that they choose. We find ourselves being a little upset about it. Someone asks you, where did you get that? How much was it? We don't want to give that information for some reason. Because we don't want someone copying us. Life is about life and no one has the true answer of what life should be and how it should be. Someone copying you should be the greatest compliment to you. Because in life, in order for us to learn life, we have to copy something. Think about it before you talk about it as if there's something wrong because you copy someone in order for your life to go on. When you admire someone and look up to them, in some ways you want to be a lot like them. So the ones that want to be like you, you shouldn't look down on them. You should be happy to tell them where you bought it, the reason why you thought about it. How much it was and where you got it.

In order for you to know what food is and know how to eat from a spoon, you have to copy someone. You have to copy the fact that your mom, your dad, someone is there to eat in front of you to show you how to eat. Someone is there to walk for you so you can mimic them, in your way, to try to walk. Someone is talking to you and changing their voice and altering their body in so many different ways that you don't understand. This is the way to say it, to do it. So in order for you to do it, you had to copy someone so you can get through it. So now that we're older and there's someone that looks up to us, sitting next to us and wanting to be like us...we find ourselves talking about them as if they can't be like us. We are not worthy of the prize to be something so different that someone else's eyes cannot achieve. So roll up your sleeves and show them that they are just like you. No matter who they are and where they are. You can tell them about your thoughts because you are you. Be happy that someone wants to be like you.

In order for you to be you, you had to mimic someone else to find you. That's life. Live up to the respect of someone wanting to live like you and walk like you so they can be like you, so someone can want to be like them and walk like them and talk like them. It's so wonderful how simple it can be when there's no seams to be seen where it is connected.

Copying

It's like poetry in motion because every wave in the ocean follows one another. No wave is ever exactly the same but they are the same because they all are waves. So let's do the best to be the best and show the rest that they can be the best so we all are the best together. True love from Above.

True love from above. Seeing us all as one.

Copying
K. Owens

My Mom

My mom is the hardest person for me to write about,
because I've never seen a word that can express
how I feel about her.
My mom is the easiest for me to write about,
because when I want to say I love her the words easily flow
between my lips.

I can talk for days because I still can't find the words to explain...
what she means to me.
She gave us when she didn't have it.
She made it happen even at times
when she felt she didn't have what it took to make it happen.
She cried alone in rooms; she didn't realize
that we heard her at times.
Hearing her voice gives me the chills even to this day.
It doesn't matter how old I am.
If I'm sitting in a different state or across the table
and I know I'm doing something wrong, I can sense it,
and just out of respect I will shut up.

My next book, God willing,
I will find the true words to let you know
what my mom means to me.
Within this time you should think about what your mom and
your parents mean to you because I only had a mom.
She was my mom and dad.
Whatever you have, think about what they mean to you.
Nobody is perfect.
The steps that everyone takes decide their fate.
Take it for what it is,
because from the start we all had to be kids in order to be adults.
We had to learn how to talk, walk swing, scream, and shout.
Let's take it for what it is.
Let's not forget about our moms.

Mama, I love you.
I know that's not the word that explains you,
but that's the only word that I know of you.
I know God would give me more strength to find different words
and different ways to say I love you
but until then, every day I will show you.
Through the phone calls...you can hear it in my voice.
Through the mail...you see it in my writing.
This book is dedicated to you.

I love you Mama.

My Mom
K. Owens

I Wonder Why

I wonder why, growing up, I didn't have a dad. He just wasn't there. All the air that I breathed, it was air that I could not share with a father. The only father that I knew was in the form of a woman. She was my mom and she was my father.

I had so many questions and I wanted to know why. I wanted to know why my hands were the way they were or my feet were the way they were. Or even the way that I walked or the way I talked or even my attitude. But whatever it was I didn't know what it was. I knew some part of me because I saw my grandma, I saw my grandpa. I saw my mom sitting and talking on the phone. Just hearing her voice in my room, I knew I wasn't alone.

Those questions that were never answered but now I finally realize what those answers are because I am in the same position where I have two sons and they are probably asking the same questions that I asked. I was the same father that I missed? So if I want to ask the question, I just look in the mirror and ask myself. And then I ask myself why.

I get tongue-tied because I don't know why. I try to pick up the phone and want to call them everyday. Sometimes I fear it and I'm scared. Some days I spend time with either my son Canaan or Matthew and every minute seems like it's an hour because I don't know what to talk to them about because I'm not used to that. I don't know that side of me. So I find myself running sometimes when I'm holding onto the phone at the same time talking to them or finding reasons to be busy versus picking them up.

I know I can be a better father and I know I will be a better father. I know I've cried many tears trying to find myself by looking at my kids or hearing their voices on the phone. I just don't want them to go through the same thing that I did. Right now I know I have the strength for them not to ever be alone. So you and I, we will take this flight. My mom and me will start us off the way we started at the beginning, and my sons will be my sons and I will be the father to them that I am supposed to be. In order for me to find that father within in me, I had to go through the father that I had seen through you, Mom, because you were the only father that I knew. I was trying to be the father that I thought a father was supposed to be because I was trying to figure out what my dad would've been like. I didn't know that so I spent so many years running from them trying to figure it out. They are losing just like I lost.

Now I realize I have to look at the only father that I've ever known, my mom and that is me. Now I realize I don't have to be anyone different, I can just be me and the father that I see within me through the mother that I've seen within me. That's the answer. I finally found the answer. Get on that plane; look him in his eyes because now I won't be ashamed.

So if there is any question to be asked, he can ask me because I'm his dad.

I wonder Why?

By

K. Owens

The Kid in You

Do you miss the kid in you?
The one that can run and play all day and never get tired?
You can sit in your room and play with toys
and have a good conversation and it's just you.
It's you talking to the kid in you.
You can put on your clothes and you didn't have to buy them.
Everything you had was given to you
and it was given to you out of love.
That's what I miss...the kid in us.

I miss being able to walk outside
and not look at the things that adults do.
I can run across the grass
and not once would I think that it needs to be cut.
Jump in the car and not once do I think
the car needs to be washed.
I think it's funny that I can write on the window with my finger,
because there is so much dirt.

The only time when I got hurt is when I fell and hit my knee
or my elbow but that was all the pain that I knew.
That was life to us...it was so fun.
The illusions that we come up with our toys are so amazing
because it was all created in our heads.
Do you miss that kid in you?
Do you laugh like you used to?
If you don't laugh like you used to,
let me remind you who you are today.

When you wake up in the morning to get out of bed...
you walk into the bathroom to brush your teeth
or either shower up.
But whatever you are doing, you're taking care of that kid.
When you are brushing those teeth,
you are not jabbing that toothbrush
in your mouth; you are brushing gently,
the way they should be brushed.
You are washing your body the way it should be washed.
In the time it takes for you to put those clothes on,
either lotion or you have none,
or you're putting your clothes on —
**you are taking care of a child that is a child
that we forgot about.**
Because when you put that lotion on your arm...
think about how gently you are putting it on.

When you put those clothes on your body...
think about what you go through
to try to find an outfit that represents you.
When you were a kid it didn't really matter that much,
because you either wanted to be a super hero,
a cowboy, a princess...
Those characters were inside of us and now what we put on
doesn't represent us.
That's what makes us forget about the kid in us.

So pay attention to what you are doing to yourself.
You feed yourself in the morning; at least I hope you do.
You feed yourself at some time during the day.
Think back from when you got up...

Everything that it took for you to get to where you are right now.

While you are reading this...

You've taken care of a child and that's a child of God.

Be grateful and thankful that you are here.

Think about how precious you are

and how you took care of yourself,

this morning and throughout your day.

Stop missing those meals.

Take the time to make the time so you can find the kid in you.

So let's laugh together, let's play together,

and let's find the kid in us.

The Kid in You

By

K. Owens

The Strength of a Woman

The strength of a woman can't be measured by any scale. No matter what ruler you have to measure it in inches, it can never be long enough. There are some men who drive in fancy cars that can loose hope for the future — just because they only work for what they have to have instead of what they need. Just the essence of a woman, even if you are not with her, makes you want to be a better man. You think more about the longevity of your decisions than just the present time. A bunch of guys hanging out — we're all talking about right now and bragging about how we're going to do it. The strength from a woman helps us be the person we say we're going to be today. When we wake up a year later, there's been progress.

When she loves, she loves you deeply. When she likes you, she just likes you, and when she adores you the world does not exist unless you're in it. That's when she's in a position of saying "I do".

Sometimes we men get confused because we want to look better amongst our friends than we really are. A woman helps us be better than the person that they see we are because we have plans for the future. What you see today is only temporary, because the wheels are in motion. We have a plan. It is about family. The strength from a woman can't help us pick up the biggest boulders or move big tree trunks but it can help us go to the drawing board and figure out a way to make a machine to help us do those things. To build a home or build a building so it can stand throughout every season. When we build something in front of a woman we want it to stand forever. When we build it for our friends it's like stacking up beer cans. It doesn't matter how long it stands; it only matters how many cans we stack before it falls.

The strength of a woman gives us insight. The passion that makes our dreams become stone so that when we build something, it stands forever. When she believes, she believes in you forever. Sometimes when we believe, we only believe from moment to moment. When you love us the way you love us and look at us the way you look at us, it makes us want to believe forever. We thank you.

For men, the strength of a woman is about how our day was today. We can get on with it once we relax and then we're able to face tomorrow. With a woman, it could be about the past month if not more that led up to today. That's why she's so emotional. Everything finally took a toll on her. She's just a little uneasy. We don't understand because we think everything is going so great. We fail to pay attention to what she said or the conversations that we've avoided to watch the game. We missed the true story to understand why she's so emotional.

They say behind every strong man there's a strong woman. That is true. A strong man is stronger because a woman helps him think more about the years to come rather than just the end of the day. A woman is strong because she believes in you. Because there's something about you that makes her stronger than she's ever been and she's willing to fight for it. The essence of that makes you a better man. So behind every strong man is a strong woman. In reality it took the two of you to make each other strong so you can see a future.

The strength of a woman.

K. Owens

O.P.R.A.H.

Someone I've listened to over the years
and I've watched so many shows.
It's not just about the people that come on or even
what the subject is all about.
It's about the changes that she had to make
coming from poverty.
Dealing with the pain of fortune and fame,
and realizing her life would never be the same.
But through all the trials and tribulations...
her heart, her drive, is what keeps her alive.
Now that's special.
That someone can come through so much
and still be willing to give so much.
I know a lot of people turn on the TV
and they see the surroundings;
the color of the couch,
the way the hair and makeup and everything is done
and what today's subject is all about.
I see something different.
Every day is the same subject to me.
Because it's about drive when you had nothing.
It's about life when you didn't want to live.
It's about struggle.
You couldn't see a tomorrow and somehow the sun still came up.
I can see some of the pain through the smiles of the footsteps
that led up to this point
because in some ways my life has been somewhat parallel...
but that's life.

And if I can ever give an eighth of what she's given —
I'm not talking about the gifts,
I'm not talking about the smiles on people's faces,
I'm talking about, in that audience, all the different races of
people **together as one.**
Then my life will be worth the struggle that I've been through
because through this I can see through.
Sometimes it takes someone to make it through
for others to have a vision to even see through
and **I am thankful for that.**
The reason why this is called O.p.r.a.h...
is because of the years and the tears and facing all her fears.
She made it.
The most important thing about her making it,
is deep down inside she doesn't feel that she has.
There's still work to be done.
Now that's humble and that's real.
The only way a story can be written
in a way for the world to understand it
is the passion of the drive and the steps
to get through what she had to get through.
You have to pass on and go to heaven and take the class
and read it in a book that's written in stone.
That's why this is called **O.p.r.a.h.**

K. Owens

Harvest Time

Standing at the top of the mountain looking at every seed that you planted blossoming and becoming something or somebody. It's harvest time. We all need to come together and start noticing the time that is spent to bring us to where we are today. How we learn the words that we know. How we learn how to walk. Who taught us how to love? Who gave us the strength to stand? Who's given us the will to want to make a better tomorrow? Who's shown us how to be an example by loving us for who we are no matter who we are? It's harvest time.

When we all walk around and we see people in their old age, they are just getting to the point of their harvest time. It's time for them to look back and look at everything that they've done in their life. You see the best of it. So if you have a grandma, grandpa, a mother, a friend, uncle or aunt, great, great, great, or great — let's not make them wait to see the love in us, the good in us. The reasons why we go out of our way to show them that we're thankful that they had something to do with us being here. Let's be thankful for the blessings that we receive throughout the footsteps of our lives. I know it's hard to remember every blessing, but I guess the main blessing is someone loves you. Someone thought of you, and your chest is moving as we speak; your breathing. Let's not forget. It's harvest time.

It's harvest time for us all. Look around and start noticing things more for what they are and start paying more attention to the kids in the neighborhood so they don't come up missing or being misled. Start paying more attention to the speed that we drive. It just might help keep someone else alive. Let's not forget when it's time to eat, to take your medicine the right way. Let's not forget about ourselves, because when we forget about ourselves someone else feels the pain from the harvest time because they're waiting for the rain so we can get the nutrients that will start to wake us and to realize what they had to do to get us to where we are today.

So run and tell somebody. Tell your grandma how much you love her. Tell her how much you miss her even if you've see her every day this week. Your grandpa too, your mother, your father. Let's respect our elders. I guess sometimes it would be nice to say yes ma'am and yes sir, especially to those who don't mind it being said to them. Let's not forget it's harvest time. Let's give them a great view to look at from the top of the hill. Let's show them that we can grow together, we can play together. We can co-exist within the midst of all the weeds and trees. We can make a way because they made a way so we can see a day.

Have you ever paid attention to the glossiness in your grandma's eyes when she sees the kids coming over to visit? And the joy in your grandpa's footsteps and the jokes that he tells from time to time? There's a reason for that. It's because they've been there before and they see you coming up. Sometimes the glossiness is tears of happiness because you're so young and innocent. Sometimes their tears are because they know what you have to go through to get to where they are. They're just trying to make it easy on you. Trying to let you know what's around that corner. Don't do this — Don't do that — Watch out sweetheart — Be careful little man —Take care — Make sure you eat — Be true to yourself.

Put in an honest day's work for an honest day's pay. Be strong. Be somebody because we need to be somebody to show them that they are somebody because we are somebody. So it's harvest time. Grandma, Grandpa, the elders...take your time and get to the top of the hill. Look down at all of us who are reading this or hearing it being read. We are going to make some changes in our lives. Make our flowers a little brighter; make our trees a little taller. Make our shade from the trees for a purpose now. Now when we lean, we lean for a reason. So we can do it. Let's let them know it's harvest time. Let's be thankful because we know we all came from somewhere. Whatever your fate is...just believe in the heartbeat in your chest. Believe it's beating for a reason. You came into this world. You didn't need batteries, so let's give them a smile on their face. It's harvest time.

Thank you so much for those who came before us to show us their better days so we'll show you it's a great time for harvest. So view it from a distance and we'll show you the most beautiful valley that has ever been seen because we're coming together as one.

It's harvest time.

By
K. Owens

Tomorrow, Tomorrow

We all wait for tomorrow to make that phone call.

We all wait till tomorrow to get on our feet.

We are talking about tomorrow, forgetting about today.

When you really think about it, tomorrow really never comes.

Today, 11:59, waiting for tomorrow...**tomorrow never comes.**

Because when the clock strikes twelve, it becomes **today.**

So now we can say tomorrow once again.

So tomorrow need never be used in the sense

that you are going to change

or you're going to do something different

or make bigger goals tomorrow.

Somehow it would be best first saying...

we started our goals today,

we are going to finish our goals today, we can find out how to

make a way because today is the only day that we can live in...

it is today.

Today only has a yesterday, and there's no tomorrow to follow,

because tomorrow never comes if you really think about it.

So let's try to get today right.

Let's make sure that we're the best that we can be.

Let's try to do our best not to judge and look at people differently.

Just because our neighbors are different religions,

drive different cars,

have different goals — doesn't make them any better or any less

than what we are because we all are living in today.

We are not promised tomorrow

because if we were promised tomorrow,

it would be a promise that never comes true

because tomorrow always becomes today.

So let's not wait until tomorrow...**today is the day.**

By
K. Owens

Yesterday and Today

I thank Thee for giving me yesterday.

I thank Thee for the air that I breathe

and for the buttons that are on my sleeve.

I thank Thee for the strength that it took to put on my shoes.

And I thank Thee for the option to choose.

I thank Thee for yesterday and today.

Because those are the days that I have

and I pray for my tomorrow and my days to come.

Give me the visions to see everyone as one.

My brother, my sister, my best friend.

I thank Thee for forgiving us for our sins.

By
Kelly Owens

Making Love

The best love ever made is in the making.
It's just something simple, just a phone call or a whisper in someone's ear
or the chills that you feel all over your body just because they are near.
Making love by just looking at them, just seeing what's really in their eyes.
It's not all about your hips and your thighs.
It's about you...
Someone putting their hand on your shoulder or just giving you a hug.
That's real love...

Making love isn't a process.
When you are making something and doing something for someone else
and it's for no reason — it's just because you love them.
That's what making love is all about...
It's about the times when you want to scream and shout
and you hold your tongue...
Or the feeling that someone gives you just by thinking of them.
Like flowers for no reason; gifts don't necessarily have to be flowers.
The gift can be a card that's left on your windshield.
It can be a book called Can You Imagine.

It can be a tie lying on top of your dresser
or a pair of boots or a pair of heels.
Those are the moments when your heart skips a beat.
Because you are making yourself be within someone else,
and it's not physical...
It can be just what you said or how you said it.

Finding love when you are in a room with others
and they can see that you love one another
just by the smile on your face, the confidence in your walk, the
tone of your voice.
That's love.Because you are making it happen.
You are making LOVE happen.
When you hear that key open the door,
you are not keeping score of who did this and who did that.
Because it's about you. It's about them, it's about love.
You are making it. Running, chasing someone for no reason.
Laughing when something is not funny but it is funny
just because the look that he or she had on their face.
We miss those things...
Somehow or another we forgot that making love is
more about what you do when you do what you do,
when you love someone the way they love you.
That's love.

Look from the corner of your eyes; you can see a shadow
or you can smell the cologne or perfume
or just sense when that person walks in the room.
You are complete with how you feel because that love is real.
Embrace the moments that you have when you are apart.
When you are standing next to each other just holding hands.
Notice the texture of each other's fingertips.
Notice the way that person walks.
Notice how you walk differently because they are a part of you.
The confidence within your strut.
Now that's making true love...

Love is something when it's instant.
You don't have to think of it, it just happens.
When someone asks a question, you answer before they finish.
It's not about the bedroom or the living room
It's about the room that you made for each other,

when you are outside within the world in those big spaces.
Because most people can only find love in small places,
because the small places make them focus on each other.

Real love — you can stand in the middle of a football field
and he or she can be in a different football field in a different state
—
You feel the love as if it's just right there because that's faith.

Let's pray for those old days to be new days
so we can be crazy for that love and reach up for that love.
Ready to make things happen because it's real.
Real love comes from heaven, your heart, your spirit,
your smile, your touch, your walk, your swagger,
your grin, your friend, your relationship.
Can you feel that???
If you can that means that you are in love.
Don't forget about the small things
that led up to the big picture...
to where you are now.
Preserve that real love.
Don't waste it.

Making Love

By

K. Owens

Headed to Heaven on the Airline

As a little kid growing up, there are so many things and so many routes that you can take just trying to find your way or find out the purpose of life. I view it as walking up to an airport. As a little kid walking to an airport and each airline represents a different religion: Delta, Southwest, Continental. There are so many airlines that you can choose or so many religions you can choose. How do you choose?

I walk up to the airline as a little kid and the airline is so huge to the point where I'm more confused than anything because I don't know which airline to go to. I'm just trying to get to a certain place and each place is the cost of a ticket, but is my ticket to heaven the price of a ticket? Do I go to the cheapest airline because I want to get there? Because where I'm trying to go is to heaven's gates? Do I go to someone that offers me a ticket for the cheapest price or first class or someone who has a medium price or whether their plane looks bigger than the other plane? I don't know. I just want to get to heaven, but I know I need to get to heaven on one of these airlines. There are so many. I can look up at the screen and I can see fifteen different airlines. Jumbo jets, tall planes. For some reason they all just seem the same because when I look at this television screen that tells you who arrives and when they arrive and when they depart, they are all getting there. Each plane for some reason is arriving at its own destination.

I can walk up to the counter with just a little money in my pocket. The lady can tell me it's going to cost me this. I go to another one and a guy tells me it's going to cost me that. How do I choose my faith when they all seem the same? And they all are offering me the best package to get me there? So is it all about the comfort of the surroundings that I have when I'm in flight? Or is it all about me standing there flat-footed looking at the big counter and those big words that are going across the sign saying what time they land and what time they take off? I'm trying to find me. Where is it for me to be? Where is it for me to be where I can fly free?

I don't think going to heaven should cost me anything out of my pocket. It should cost me what I've put in my soul while I was here. But the airport is so big, I fear it. Because if I go sit on one airplane, I don't want to not understand the other. Either way they all have their own purpose, but somehow they all get there. I just want to get to heaven on this airline, and I feel confused so I can drop to my knees and just cry. I don't want to just die and be alone. I want to get on the plane and I want to get on the right one that will take me home. There are so many different beliefs, so many different desires.

I look and I see a sign that says we are willing to hire. I don't need a job, I just want to get home. All these people pulling their bags, some happy, some sad. They all are getting on different planes for different reasons. I don't know what that reason is, I'm just trying to find me. So I'm going to heaven and I'm going to make it. I'm going to close my eyes when I pass that door. I'm not going to keep score of who says this and who says that. I'm going to walk up to the first counter that I feel with my fingertips when my eyes are closed and I'm going to say "Get me home". I'm ready to go home and I'm on my own. So I say "Get me home".

Get me home because my life is not about the price of a ticket. The price that I've paid for all the things that I've been through in my life and the decisions that I've made to be able to get here. Being able to say no when other people wanted me to say yes. Being able to say yes when I know it's the best for me. I'm working on getting myself together so I can get home. When I walk in this airport it's not about a ticket or the price of a ticket. It's about me and who I am or what I had to go through just to walk through those doors. When I walk through those doors I'm not looking at religion. I'm not looking at race. I'm not looking at what plane is going to get me to that place. The thing that matters to me is that this is the place that I know I need to be to get home. Flying free on the wings. On what airline it doesn't matter because I can close my eyes and I can hear the angels sing. To heaven I go and I'm on my way. Does it matter to me the name that's on the outside of that plane? Does it matter to me? It doesn't matter to me, because the only thing I see is the heaven within me.

Headed to Heaven on the Airline

By

Kelly Owens

Can You Imagine?

Can you imagine growing up being a carpenter?

Can you imagine when everything that you spoke of...some people believed you and some didn't? The reason why you were loved so much; you were hated for the same reason.

Can you imagine giving your life and everything that you believed in just to be here?

To go through your whole life for change and to be able to show a better life in that there is life and there is love, and a love to be loved and showing love is the reason for love.

Can you imagine being for the greatest good and still being wrong in people's eyes?

Can you imagine at the point of changing so many lives and having so many followers and having so many people who believe that you are the one that had to roll up your sleeves to give your own blood? Can you imagine?

Today we deal with cancer, AIDS, diabetes, and everything else, but can you imagine the way it was in the biblical sense?

Can you imagine carrying something so heavy your knees buckle?

Can you imagine looking from the side of your eyes with tears and you can barely see a friend who used to be a friend?

Can you imagine changing people's lives so much so they can have so much glory but when you are in a time of need, all they can say is I'm sorry?

Can you imagine the pain of having something two, three, maybe even four times your weight and carrying it on your back just to preserve everyone else's faith?

Can you imagine having blood coming from every vein in your body from being whipped just to carry on to give people a reason to live on? Can you imagine?

Can you imagine carrying something on your back that is so heavy that what you are carrying dents the ground in such a deep thrust that it takes weeks for the rain and mud to cover it up?

Can you imagine being humble and willing to forgive those people who were throwing rocks and spitting just because they didn't understand.

Can you imagine the pain when it seems as if it's about to rain and it's just the blood that's coming from your veins?

And you still have a humble heart where you don't see things in the dark. Can you imagine?

Can you imagine dragging what you have on your back? You had to carry it so far but you made it anyway.

Can you imagine looking from the corner of your eyes seeing the woman who bore you and brought you into this world crying at the top of her lungs and she can't do anything to help you?

Can you imagine the strength to lift something that you couldn't but you lifted it anyway?

Can you imagine getting to the top of the hill and being crucified on the cross?

Can you imagine the big stakes being stabbed in your hands and pierced in your side and you still have the will, with tears in your eyes to say, "Father, forgive them for they know not what they do"? Forgive them for their sins. Can you imagine?

And if you have a friend that loves you that way, I would say you believe everything that they say forever and a day. If not, I'm going to follow my friend, my father who has forgiven us forever and a day. Can you imagine?

Can you imagine what it took just to get there?

Can you imagine the life that he had here and what he had to share?

Can you imagine the last thoughts that he had when he breathed his last breath?

Can you imagine that he asked his father to forgive us and let us live on?

Can you imagine?

If you can imagine, you're heaven sent.

If you can imagine, you believe in this.

Jesus is Jesus, and he came here to forgive us for our sins, but he walked the earth the way we walk the earth.

He was a carpenter to be able to show us what true hard work was all about.

Throughout his life all he heard were people screaming and shouting, but he still forgave us for our sins. If you could follow the legacy of the life that he lived, you have the will to get in.

So I pray, Heavenly Father, in Jesus's name, give us the strength to know...

Give us the strength to not have doubt.

Give us the will to know when it's time to scream and shout.

Give us whatever it takes for us to stand as a woman and a man.

Give us what it takes to look in our child's eyes and to make the right decisions by the time we wipe the tears from their eyes.

Give us the strength to carry the burden of our lives through these earthly steps that we have to take to get to heaven's gates.

Gives us the strength to forgive when we don't know how to forgive.

Give us the strength to understand even when we don't understand.

Give us the will and the reason to want to live on.

Give us the knowledge to help our minds filter all the bad things that go through our mind. Father, we come to you with our knees on the ground, hands to our face to praise because of you we have our happy days, we have our sad days, but we have days.

Whatever days we have, let it be the days that we give praise. We understand and we know what it took for you to walk this land.

Give us the will and the humble heart to be able to get there and still be willing to share.

In the Lord, Jesus Christ's name we pray, Amen.

Can You Imagine

By
Kelly Owens

Born Again

Live your life as if there was no yesterday…
but let yesterday give you the strength to conquer
your tomorrows.

By

K. Owens

Guiding Light

Dark and cloudy day.
Only through you I can see the sunshine and on a cold
and winter day I feel warm inside.
When the sun is bright as it can be, I feel your shade
protecting me.
When I'm down on my luck you inspire me to never
give up.
I can feel your presence surrounding me.
Thank you for taking your time creating me.

By
K. Owens

The World We Live In

The world we live in...we have the technology to see a license plate from thousands and thousands of miles away, but for some reason we don't have the technology to walk up to that same person and wish them a better day. Two people who are leading their countries can't get along. Thousands and thousands of people lose their lives just because those two are pointing fingers and saying someone is wrong. Is that the world we live in today?

We have computers that can figure out every problem mathematically, can find any address, and can search for miles and miles for a handbag that you don't see in stores. At the same time we have people who live right next to each other and have no idea what each other's last name is. Is that the world we live in today?

I've seen many places that are being built and have designs that cost millions and millions of dollars. I see extra work being done on places just to make them look a little bit better. But you can barely see the work that is done to help people feel better. Is that the world we live in today?

Our technology can fly planes around the world. Our attitude keeps us within our own world, and our own world is just standing above the two feet that are beneath us. Why can't we change too? The technology that we have should be about us getting to know each other better. We can lose just a little bit of the technology that tells us about the weather if we learn together how to weather the storm no matter what the day is all about.

Seeing people rushing to work trying to get there on time. Cell phones are ringing, people are talking, life is changing, but technology is so much further than we are. How can we be so blind to be able to sit at a desk and create something that is so much further advanced then we are? We are sitting at the same desk, too lazy to get up to get our own cup of coffee. Is that the world we live in today?

Our world should be all about boys and girls. When you think about boys and girls you see the beauty of life. It makes you think about the future. When you think about adults, you think their time has already been spent and they've lived a good life or somewhat of a good life up to that point. We don't realize that the adults are the ones who hold the puzzle together in order for the boys and girls to have safe places to play. To be able to cross over the lines to find new lives and new joy with each other.

This world that we have can't change unless we change. The technology on the TV and in your light switch and the car you drive is so much more advanced than our attitudes, and that shouldn't be the world that we live in today. We need to be more advanced than our computers; more advanced than our TVs. HD and the clearest channels should be about you and me finding each other. That's the world we need to live in today.

The two people who lead their countries need be able to sit down and talk about things and not just politics. Talk about their families and the reason why they are in the positions that they are. Maybe they can find something within each other that reminds them of life's purpose. No life need be lost over a misunderstanding. When it's all about politics nothing ever lines up because everyone has an opinion. When it's all about family it's all the same because everybody has the same purpose. Reach out for the air that is right in front of your face. Rub your hands in your eyes and do not think about what color or what race. Take a deep breath and you'll realize that you are living. Take a chance for change because the change could be changing you and others. Slow down just a little bit and you'll see the beauty that is unfolding right before you.

Let's help each other find the world that we should be living in today, so it's the world we live in always.

By K. Owens

I was scared

I didn't want to like you too much,

So I pushed you away.

I loved you silently.

Being vulnerable is something that I feared.

Each time I hung up the phone

I felt like calling you back,

But I didn't.

I waited for the phone to ring

for hopes that it was you.

And when it did, and it wasn't,

I was mad at the person who did call,

just because.

And when you called,

I said "I have something else to do".

I found every excuse to push you away and now I'm realizing it goes as far back as my childhood.

I love the kid in you but when I was younger, I always had to play alone, so I had to find happiness within myself and I'm trying to open up to play with someone else.

The adult in you makes me want to cry because when I see you being serious, it reminds me how I was talked at instead of talked to as a kid. Even though the serious side of you was so sweet, it scared me just a bit.

My instincts were to protect myself and run away.

And while I was away I found more excuses because

you didn't come chasing or come knocking at my door.

When I was a child, I ran away sometimes and what made me feel love is when they came looking for me. And now that I think about it, you have no idea what I've been through or any idea where I live. Sometimes, I close my eyes calling you in my sleep hoping you can find where I'm hiding even though I'm not far away.

I want to face my vulnerable side, not just for you,

I'm going to do it for me.

This is the beginning of an ending.

I've cried about my past and now it's time for me to live for the future.

Falling in love with you silently and losing you emotionally and physically has made me, for the first time in my life, realize I'm facing my greatest loss of losing you and my biggest gain of finding me.

The key to my heart does exist now that I realize why I keep doing this; pushing you away and expecting you to be able to read my mind and know exactly how I am feeling.

And now I am willing to express how I feel and I'm sad to know you have moved on

because I have finally found the key to the door that's always been shut.

And most importantly, I realize when I fold my arms and walk away,

my mouth is the door that has always been closed.

My door is open.

My heart is humble.

My mind is troubled from the past.

Wishing I could do it all over again.

The sound of your voice or just the thought of you gives me the chills

when it's a hundred degrees.

I never knew my feelings for you were so deep until I heard that you had moved on.

And I know it's selfish of me so I don't want to run. I want to face the pain and be happy for you because things have to change.

The hardest words I've ever had to say, I'm sorry, I was scared

I was scared

By K. Owens

When the Day Comes

Your parents have raised you up through school to be strong and taught you how to follow the rules - rules to understand life. Take the lessons you've learned and don't stray away from your family values. Your family is your family. You can be happy with, or you can be happy without, but either way, something is wrong if you don't take the future and your past and put them together to make one.

A mother, a father, building a home and making room for the ones they raised so they know they always have a place where they can come home. Empty space that hasn't been filled. There's plenty of space for two people to shed tears. You can't forget the family that you have after all the struggles and coming up through school and finding yourself. Kids keep forgetting what you've taught them. No matter what life we find, when we seek adulthood we can't forget how we got there in the first place.

Don't let an empty room stay an empty room at your parents' home. Let it be a room that you and your new family plan to stay in soon. Show your husband or wife the parents who are your true friends. They taught you tough love from the beginning. Even if it's a stepparent, the love is still real. All your happy days of living together, your parents pray for those happy days to be better days even if it's not days lived for them. Don't forget. The next time you look at a calendar to make plans with your partner, choose a vacation. Out of respect for the family who sacrificed so much so you could stand on your own at least once a year.

You are a beautiful flower growing in this world. Eager to see everything there is to see. Confused by life and short moments and willing to give life when the moments are right. Just don't forget those that gave you life. Those days when you pray for better days just remember someone was praying for you before your days even existed.

Can you feel your heart beating? Can you feel memories of the past? Are your thoughts within thoughts when you're thinking about things that you can do differently? The love that you have gained when you've become older can be even more and greater when you reach back for the love that has given you love. Give back, take back, a minute or two and remember the ones that took time out of their lives and sacrificed so you can be you. When you have kids, you want your kids to follow the footsteps that you've made. If your footsteps are not leading to the footsteps of those who have raised you in this world today, then you shouldn't be disappointed, when your kids get older, if their footsteps do not follow your way.

Be an example. Don't forget the love. All the love and the love that was given to you so that you could be you. Give back so the kids that you do have, have an example to follow. When they give back they'll give back to you. When the day comes and you have kids, don't forget Grandma and Grandpa.

By,
K. Owens

Blind Faith

Blind Faith. It's like a seed falling on the ground or getting planted.

One way or another, life begins.

When you are so deep in the ground you can't see light,

your faith that you have gives you the will to fight,

gives you the strength to reach for the light.

As that seed is coming up from the ground it has to have faith.

By the time it breaks the ground, there will be life.

It's just like in our own lives.

Sometimes you can't see it. It doesn't mean that it's not there.

So just think about when a seed is coming up through the ground.

The darkness, dirt, and every other challenge...

the strength it needs to push it away, to make a way.

It makes a way because it knows that God will give it light to grow.

By the time it gets to the surface it reaches as high as it can to get to the sun.

Throughout the life of growing you find many things that you have to deal with...

The bad weather, the ups and downs — but you strive to make it.

Some people don't make it through the storm, so prepare yourself.

but if you can read this you are one of the ones that made it.

You are one of the ones who is growing and reaching.

When a flower gets to the peak, overcoming all its struggles...

It opens slowly and it shows you the most beautiful colors to tell you its story.

When it blooms at its peak, that's when it's the most vulnerable.

So make sure when you get to that point,

you have the strength to live on and reach on.

The sun, life, and the weather are giving us all what it takes to weather the storm.
Reach out to your friends and families so you can have someone to lean on,
because sometimes we can't grow alone.
We have to grow together so we can weather the storm together.
When the wind blows, some of us are catching the wind
of the flower that is next to us; that is our friend.

Believe that you can achieve the light that has been given to you.
Reach for light and for life that is your life, to make it the most beautiful picture
the eyes have ever seen because of the struggles that you had to go through...
to get to where you are.
Show God that you are worthy when it's time for you to go home.
Paint that picture, show those colors, and reach out for life's light.
Show the flower next to you what the color is supposed to be like.
When you look over and see that their colors are different than yours
just realize that you together, have the most beautiful picture,
and you made it through the weather. Surround yourself with good people and good values so your purpose alone will be something to follow, even if blindfolded. Because it's blind faith.

Let's show the world that once we were blind and now we can see.
We are not just a seed, we live and we breathe. Now we can change life
so we can have life and we can give life.

Blind Faith

By K. Owens

Can I?

Can I be honest with you?

Can we talk?

Can we take time when there's no time from within our hearts

so we can find a time?

Can we talk?

Can we talk about the past and find solutions for the future?

Can I say I'm sorry now for what's to come

even when I don't know it, because I know I'm not perfect? Can

I?

Can I walk with you? Can I smell what you have on? Can I hold

your hand? Can I?

Can I pick up a book and read it to you and the book is called,

Can You Imagine?

Can you imagine that we made it this far?

Can you imagine that our heart is still beating even when there

are no batteries?

Life is life and we give each other a reason to want to live?

Can I feel your spirit? Can I feel what you possess within your

soul? Can I?

Can we be as one when we do what we do,

because it's not about me and it's not about you, it's about us.

Can I?

Can I take a chance of a little dance and a little romance

and it has nothing to do with finance?

Can I?

Would you love me the same if I either had or had not?

Would you love me the same?

Can I ask you a question?

Can you love me the way I love you?

Can I take the time to find the time to hear your points

of telling me about the times that brought you here?

Can I?

Can we both find the reason why we exist and give praise to it?

Can we reach to the heavens together...

with the strength within both of our arms, hearts beating, and

souls reaching?

Spirit with so much joy and love to give, which gives us the

reason to want to live?

Can we do it as one?

So when I say can I...can I, stands for us. Because **we are one**.

So I'm saying can I?

Can I whisper something in your ear that will send chills

through all your friends, families and the people that don't know

you?

Can I? Can we? Can you?

Can I find the time to cry for past times, reaching for the

good times, saying goodbye to the bad times with the will to

overcome life after life?

Can I?

Can I ask our heavenly father truly what is your heaven-sent name and what is mine?

And don't forget when I say can I, **we are as one.**
So we are saying, can we, for **we are as one so we shall say, can I.**
Can I ask the heavens to open because the day comes soon for us to go home?
Can I walk hand in hand to the gates? Can I?
Can I say good day, good night, good evening, good love, goodbye, don't cry.
Can I?
Can you whisper in my ear?
Can you tell me a secret?
Can we be we, us be us, me be you and you be I and I be one?

Can I?

True to a heart that is given in a spiritual sense...Can I?

K. Owens

Gifts

Gifts that you receive throughout your life.

Birthdays and holidays are gifts just because. Gifts...what is a gift?

Is a gift the gift that someone has given to you? Is a gift that bicycle that's leaning against your garage or lying out there on the grass?

When someone goes to the mall or to the store to buy you something because they're thinking of you maybe it's your birthday or a holiday, the gift is not the gift that they gave to you. The gift is the time that they spent thinking of you.

The gift is the gift of life, so you got a gift just to be here.

A gift to read this, the gift to see this...that is your gift.

Let's not think about the things that fade and the things that can burn down. Let's think about the things that you feel within and feel from your heart. That is the gift.

So sometimes when you want to leave something on the dresser for someone just to make them smile, there's a true gift that was given...the gift of you giving and the gift of them receiving.

The footsteps that you take are preserved. You are searching for life and doing something right with it and changing life. So let's all give gifts. Let's take the time and find the time so we can make the time to give a gift.

What would you like? If someone asked you what you would like, would it be something that you see or something you feel? Something you feel is always real because you can carry it no matter where you go. You can get on the plane and carry it in your heart and not once be stopped by the metal detectors. Someone else can give you a gift, and if your life is about what you see, then you find yourself saying to those people — I can't take this with me. I have to check it and it has to go below.

So what is the gift? A gift you can take anywhere that you go.

If you're heart is beating...that is a gift.

If you are breathing...that is a gift.

If you can eat, speak, feel, or have skin...the gift is always your true friend.

The gift of life...So we have to have life in order to give life to receive a gift. So let's all be gift givers and let's all be gift receivers. So that is a gift and the gift is within a gift.

Gifts

By
K. Owens

How Do You Know?

How do you know if you're a great husband? How do you know if you're a great wife, girlfriend, boyfriend, friend, sister, or brother? Or you're just another — you don't have a title but you're standing by because you like to be a friend. How do you know? You know when you can see it and feel it before it can be seen or felt. When it's real it travels before a word is even spoken. You know you're loved; you know you're cared about. You just know it.

Sometimes we know it and we doubt it just because we want the other person to shout it and we need to stop that. Real love is real love no matter how it's shown and no matter what shelf it's on.

When it's real, it's real.

So how do you know it?

You know it when you are a great friend, husband, wife, sister, brother, grandma, grandpa, step dad, or real dad. You just know it. You know you're doing your best and you don't complain about the rest. If you think it needs to be done, it's done. If you want to say I love you it's already been said. It's embedded in your soul. How do you know that you are great beyond great and that you are loved beyond loved? You just know it. You don't complain as much. You give tough love when you know real love needs to be shown. You care more about how people see the people that you care about than how they see you. You're willing to step up to the plate and say what you think is right. When it's time to gossip about someone — what he said or she said — you hold your tongue because you know it's not right.

So how do you know it? You just do.

How do you know it?

K. Owens

Crying

Why do we cry?
Why do we fight the tears?
Why do we try to hold them back and not let it out?
Is it that we are ashamed about what we are crying about?
Why do we cry?
I cry sometimes because life is hard.
It's hard making the right decisions all the time.
It's hard to make a wrong decision when
you had a choice to make the right decision...
but you didn't.
I'm crying because some of my decisions are right but the
hardest to go through, so I cry.
I cry a lot on the inside.
With the walls that I put up, someone usually ends up getting
hurt because I'm protecting myself
even when they've done nothing wrong.

Now I know it's okay to cry
because every day is a new challenge.
Some days I feel I have everything covered,
Then there is a phone call and it's money I don't have.
Some days I walk down the street and for no reason,
my eyes get teary and my hands open
and close from a fist to an open hand
just because I'm trying to find my way.
It's hard to find my way carrying my weight
and the weight of others.
It was easy yesterday but it is hard today.

Why do I cry?
I cry for peace, I cry for something to eat,
I cry for a pair of shoes to fit my feet.
I cry for peace to get that weight off my shoulders.
It's because that burden of pain is not so heavy anymore.
I used to be embarrassed to shed a tear.
I used to be embarrassed for things I feared.
I'm not ashamed now.
I can face it with tears in my eyes
and with strength to overcome it.
So one day I can cry again.
Cry to say goodbye to old habits, cry to old friends.
I cry when family members come in and out of town.

Is it okay to cry? I used to think not.
When I think back to every time I shed a tear,
if I was standing in a lake it would be up to my chest.
So it is okay to cry.
Every time I've cried the sun was a little brighter.
Every time I've cried the weight was a little lighter.
Every time I cried, I cried for the fact
that people have lived and had to die.
I cry for me. I cry for you.
Let's cry together so we can change the world together.
Let's not be ashamed because it's not about fortune and fame,
it's about who you are, not what you have.
It's about me, it's about you, it's about them, and it's about us.
So let's get together so we are not afraid
to change the world together.

By
K. Owens

A Great Message

Our world is crumbling right in front of us. Each day somebody has done something unthinkable. We are all searching for the positive in something. There are many great messages that are out there. You can see a movie that makes you want to change the world. You can hear a song that keeps your mind at ease. You can see world peace instead of seeing people deceased. Yes, that's a great message.

People get angry when there's no reason for them to get angry. Somebody is backing up and they don't see you and you yell at them. Now you see, so what's the purpose of rolling your eyes or flipping the finger when you're still looking? A mistake is a mistake.

There are so many messages on commercials saying stop smoking, don't do drugs, go to school, and get an education. Those are great messages. The hardest thing about reality is the best message that you get is a message that is changing on a daily basis instead of just words being said. Commercials that flash in your face for less than ten seconds. A movie that was so potent it makes you want to change the world, but after 24 hours, your world is even worse than it was before you saw the movie. That was a great message but we can say it was a temporary message. One to slow you down just a bit. To slow down statistics of what could've been. When tomorrow or the next day comes and everything is the same, now what?

I can step up and make a movie about people coming together, but once that movie is over and I've made my money and I'm off to a new production about a little girl or a boy flying a kite — what difference have I made in your life if it was just that movie? If we're going to put a message out there then we need to put something out there that reminds you of it everyday.

Life can be so much better. Commercials can be like movies because you can see the change in people's lives on a day-to-day basis. You can see the advertisements everywhere, and people are changing. It's not just minute-to-minute If someone sang a song about changing a child's' life, and after the song was sung, the artist actually gave back to that same purpose, then that song is validated. Seeing the change in that child's life makes you want to change. The best message, the true message, is a message that will continue after the message is delivered. Let's just show a little more passion about what we are singing, writing, and producing. Just put a little bit back out there so people can actually see it in their neighborhoods. It would be so amazing having someone read your book twice just because they can see you making changes every day. Watching your movie four times because they can actually see somebody's life that you've changed physically. Singing a song about change and watching the news and seeing that you donated something to that very cause. Now that's change. That's a great message.

A Great Message

By

K. Owens

The Truth

We all walk around and we want the truth.
The truth is the hardest thing for us to give,
so why is the truth so important?
We need the truth.
The truth is the only way you can know someone
and for it to be real.
So let's face the truth.
If you have something on
and you ask someone how does this look?
Do you want 50 percent of the truth
or 100 percent of the truth?
If you get 100 percent of the truth
and it doesn't go in your favor,
don't be upset because you asked for the truth.
If you are upset, tell that person the percentage of the truth that
you're searching for.
Fifty percent, 75 percent, or 100 percent.
Be consistent with the truth that you want
and be willing to accept the answer.

Or just be 100 percent!

If you owe someone something, the truth is that you owe them.
If it goes on so long to the point where they say your
relationship is more important than the loan that was made,
then the truth is, you are wrong because you didn't pay it back.
Most of us that owe, are driving new cars, in new homes,
and are talking on cell phones,
and for some reason we can do no wrong.
We always have excuses for not returning the favor.

When your phone rings, and you know who's calling and you
ask someone else to pick it up and say...You're not there.
Is asking them to lie...Truth?
The truth is there is no truth in that.
The truth is answering the phone, facing it,
saying no, yes, whatever it is, but *you* deal with it...

Or...just don't answer

That's the truth.

When you tell someone your going to do something that needs
to be done today and you put it off to another day, then you
have to wait for that day to come for today's lie to become truth.

Let's be truthful to ourselves.

The truth should be told written in stone.
Being able to admit when you are wrong.
That's one of the reasons why it's hard for us
to believe that we can achieve greatness in life.

**Because sometimes in our little mistruths,
we find ourselves doubting the truth.**

Because when it's said, we feel as if we are being misled
and it could've been the truth from the start.
So what would you rather have?
If you tell all of your friends the truth all the time,
you'll have half the friends that you have now.
Is it better to have half the friends and have them true friends?
Or all your friends and there's no truth in them?
So be a friend and tell the truth.

My mom called me this morning and asked me —
did you go to church?
Instantly I wanted to say yes
but I realized it was just a test after writing this...
so I told her the truth.
And it wasn't so bad.
She did get mad that I didn't go...
I don't have to cover up for the truth.
Now I can face her and look her in the eyes
because I told the truth.

None of us are perfect.
The best things in life are hard to accept.
The worse things in life we want to fabricate
to make them seem better.
Those are the reasons why we get hurt sometimes
going in a situation
thinking that it's better than what it is.
Because it was fabricated from the beginning,
to make you feel a little bit more secure.
It's best to know what battle you are going into.
So be a true friend and tell the truth from the beginning.
So when there is an end, no matter how it goes,
you know you have a true friend.

Let's pray and ask our Heavenly Father to help us all understand
what the truth is and how to speak the truth
so we can use our tongue and teach the young.
Show them by example that there is truth.
When we say — I will be there, I'm on the way,
I will call, yes I did, No I didn't...
It will be done.
So let's pray for that because we all are one.
So I will be going to church on Sunday; you should too.
Let's make a change because change starts
with you, me, all of us...
so we all can tell the truth the next time we're asked.

The Truth

K. Owens

I Want to Live that Dream

I want to live that dream of living the dream. Things that you talk about, you're actually living. Things that you've said, you've actually done. What you're working on with people on are things that you've already built. I want to live that dream. I don't necessarily want a perfect dream, but I want it to be a dream. I want to dream to be able to fall and not feel the pain because I know that I'll soon heal.

I want a dream that is real. Something that I can touch. Something that is tangible but it's like a dream because I can't believe that it's happening. I want to dream of someone being a part of me or me being a part of them. Or being able to pray or laugh or run like there's no tomorrow. I can cry and at the same time be so happy or I cry just because. I want to live that dream.

Do you want to live that dream?

I want to live the dream when you can walk outside of your house and you can have every flower that you've ever liked planted in your yard. Or you can walk outside of your house and go to your neighbor and you can hug them around their neck and they love you too. I want to live that dream. I want to be a father that my child looks up to and says they would like to be like. I want to live that dream. I don't necessarily want it to just be me being anything great, I just want my life and what is meant — to be great. I want the purpose of my life to be great. I want to live that dream.

I want to live the dream of being able to sit at home and pick up the phone and call anyone that you know past or present and you can have a phone conversation with them as if you are brothers and sisters. There's no harm done because the past is the past and the future is the future. I want to live that dream. I want to live the dream where you can walk outside and talk to any of the kids and tell them what they should and should not do and be respected because you've been there before and the parents understand.

I want to live the dream where our families can stay in the same state and if they are not, they can't wait to get home to pick up the phone just to call you and tell you that they miss you. That's a dream to me and I want it to be reality. I want a dream where your loved one, or anyone who is dear to you, loves you the way that you love them and you know it, you feel it. You can breathe it and taste it on your tongue. You can feel as if you're a kid again because that flower is reborn through Christ and through them.

Your love is so different because now when you see a flower you see the beauty of it. You don't just see the space that it covers by putting it somewhere just to make decoration. You want it to be there because it has a purpose. That's the kind of dream I want. I want to live that dream.

My dream is to be able to breathe the air and it not be harmful to me, or my kids, or my friends, or even someone that I don't know. That's a dream to me. I would pray for the air to be free and for whatever anyone's dream is to be, they can pray and it will come true. Your blessings don't always come in the way that you want but will always, come in the way that you need.

My dream is at the end of the day to be able to lie down in my bed and close my eyes with peace. If I die and I don't wake up, I can die with a smile on my face because I'm okay. If I have a chance to wake up again to see light and breathe the air, I have another chance to change something or someone or myself. That is my dream. My dream is for me, we, to be us at all times.

Life is not about the shoes you fill; it's about the lives that you change through the footsteps that you take. That's my dream.

You live your legacy so therefore you are living your dream.

I want to Live That Dream

By
Kelly Owens

My Fairytale World

If life were like a fairytale world, it wouldn't matter whether we all get along, because we would live forever. I can walk outside and get hit by a car and get up and walk again. Walk by a graveyard and just say, its time to get up and live again. I can run from state to state to visit all of my family in one pair of shoes because it wouldn't matter — it's a fairytale. I can look across the street and my neighbors will love me or not like me, it wouldn't matter. Nothing changes because they can't hurt me. If they put a bomb in the backseat of my car and it blows up, I can get out and wipe the darkness off. I can jump in a plane and fly around the world to change the world. That can be my fairytale. You can tell everyone in the world that you love him or her at the same time. You can go to the top of the mountain and scream it at the top of your lungs. The ground will rumble the sounds of "I love you" and "Let's change the world" and "We can do it together". Now that's a fairytale. We can all eat at the same table, all of us. We can eat at the same table, same meal, at the same time. That's my fairytale. We can all kneel down and pray, asking God to come save us today. We can all do it at the same time. That's my fairytale.

Have you ever thought what life would be like if we were cartoons? Would it matter if we love each other or not? Would it matter what color we were? Would it matter if we were dinosaurs or talking cars or just rocks rolling out in the desert? Would it matter whether you were a turtle or a rabbit? It wouldn't matter how fast you were or how slow you can go because in cartoon life, no matter how slow you go, you still get there. No matter how fast you run, you still get there. No matter what color, how tall or short, you still get there. That's cartoon life.

I wish life were like a cartoon because every family member can fit in my living room. All my friends can line up and be around the world end to end. Everyone will be a true friend; that's a cartoon. I would love to have a world like that where you can walk outside and think of a pair of roller skates and magically they appear on your feet. You can think of sending flowers and you don't have to pay for delivery. You can think about the love you have in your heart and people can see it beating through your chest. That would be such a wonderful world.

In a fairytale, cartoon life, you and I, all of us, would be heaven sent because no matter what we do, we can't hurt one another. We will all live as if we are living forever. We can go back to the Flintstones, back when the dinosaurs talked. We can fly if we tie a sheet around our neck. We can be as strong as ever by eating spinach like Popeye. We can pick up buildings and move them from state to state or make a homemade spaceship and fly to heaven's gates. That, to me, would be a wonderful world.

Can you see what I see when you see the cartoon in me?

Can you see it? If you can, you are already there.

My Fairytale World

Kelly Owens

He/She

I bear witness to your friend who has controlled so many people's lives. He/she has all the answers when within the grip of your fingertips and he/she is more powerful than your mind at this moment. I have witnessed your friend being past around and given false dreams. Every time you are together you act like you are the life of the party and nothing matters.

From the outside looking in, he/she is with all your friends. He/she is only faithful to your illusions and unfaithful to the consequences of your actions. I am just telling you as a friend, you are changing. It's like you are believing in a ghost because the next day you can barely remember where you have been and he/she is like a ghost, because no one has your alibi when you decided to drive home. Your breath is a little different and I still get a rush of where you have been last night and even when you use soap or gargle there's still no hope because he/she exists within your eyes. Your body is not the same and each time you say you are not going to see he/she anymore it is a birth of a lie because now you hide it when it is so present.

I am here as a witness to say your friend is draining the life out of you right in front of your eyes. I've only seen he/she hiding behind a glass and asking for ice when it is cold inside.

On the days when you know he/she is too strong you find a chaser to chase he/she along so it doesn't have to fall hard, it falls easy.

How could you make it easier for he/she to stay? Why do you stay faithful to he/she who is unfaithful to you?

I took it upon myself to do an investigation of this he/she that has many names and I found out the name and he's not a he and she's not a she. I caught up with he/she and poured her and him down the drain. And the real name of this imposter, dream taker, smooth talker, straight up liar is called ALCOHOL and his best friend is DRUGS.

He is not a he and she is not a she.

By
K. Owens

Happy Birthday

Today is a good day for you. This is the first day that you become you. A lot of people don't realize what Happy Birthday means. Happy Birthday is all about the time that it took you to get here. It took nine months. Throughout those nine months you heard so many voices. You couldn't see any faces. The stomach was rubbed from time to time just to get through moments and to get you here. Someone has altered their lives to be uncomfortable, ornery, or whatever it was. They did what it took to get you here. The journey of being tucked in and taken care of and getting what you needed with no effort, now that's love.

Happy Birthday. For all the ups and downs throughout pregnancy, something great came out of it. By the time you came and breathed fresh air for the first time it was Happy Birthday to you because it was all about you. NO matter how much pain or what anyone went through to get you here, it was all about you! So I say to you, Happy Birthday.

Even then, you heard voices but you still couldn't see. Happy Birthday means someone picked you up and held you close. They didn't care if you were wet or dry, all they heard was your cry or the little noises that you would make so they held you close. That's Happy Birthday.

Your Happy Birthday started when someone took the responsibility of making sure you were fed and you were led in the right direction. Taking the time to change your diaper and to comfort you when nothing was wrong and you were crying anyway. Happy Birthday to you. The times when you were crying in your bed and someone had to make sure they were there to show you the way and made a way for you to see this day. This day is special because it's not about gifts. The gift that you get is that you are here and you were thought of. If you rewind time one incident could have changed your fate. Someone could have missed the bus or slipped and fell or missed a phone call and your fate could have been different, but you are here so it is Happy Birthday.

Let's say the gift is a gift that people will give to us on their own and a gift is a gift to us that we are living. We are alive, and breathing, we are doing it; that's what Happy Birthday means. Happy Birthday means you can finally see that you have been given the gift of life. It was on your birthday that you received the gift.

For the rest of your life, you need never forget that's what it is all about. You making change because one day you have to do the same. You have to have Happy Birthday for someone else. Whether you're male or female, whether you choose to have or have not. If you do choose, you will be in the same shoes of caring for someone the same way that you were cared for. Nurturing them every step that you take is preserving their fate.

So believe in yourself whether the birthday you're turning is one, five, eighteen, twenty-five, thirty, fifty, sixty, or beyond. The gift is that you had one. So let's all look at birthdays in a different way and on our birthday, the ones that we need to thank; we should be on our knees thanking God that we made our way and thanking our mothers for making their way and carrying us for those months. The passion she went through; there isn't a word to explain. On your birthday we need to give a gift of thanks to our moms for their gift of life.

If you ever want to shed a tear and you feel like you're alone on your birthday, you have to realize you are not alone on your BIRTHDAY. So you think about that!

HAPPY BIRTHDAY TO YOU.

By
Kelly Owens

Chapter 1

Windows of Life

When I look out of the window of my home, my life, I see a path lined with flowers. The people in my life who bless me with their love and let me love them back. Each flower has its special meaning for me; one is friend, one is mother, one is brother, sister, grandmother. I see the beauty in the flowers with grateful eyes. We are connected, though each has its own individual cycle of growth.

There is one I see, growing there reaching toward the sky, whose heart is pure, whose perfume is a sweet soothing balm to the senses. I stretch out my hand and instantly draw back; this one must not be picked just now.

How can I tell you, Precious Flower, that in this moment I can only stare and must look away? How do I say it is not enough for me to snip you from your place only to stand you in a water-filled jar to wait and wither and die? I am a man beneath the snow, unready to open myself, and you require nothing less. I will not pick you unless I have grown back into the light. Unless I can take you carefully from your roots, carry you inside, and press you into the book of my life forever.

Until then, I must be glad you are on my path at all, in the soil and sun and rain, where you go on growing in spite of me. Until then, I can only give thanks that as I move forward ever so slowly, I can catch your fragrance on a healing breeze. If I cannot offer you my life's pages in the midst of my own preparation time, if I cannot give you promises of what the future may hold, will you yet grant me the right to stop along the walk, gaze fully at your upturned face and tell you that you are beautiful?

Chapter 2

Windows of Life

I see the beautiful flowers, knowing that none of these could exist without the beauty from Above. Looking into the sky out of the same window, I can feel the joy from Above. What the sun, rain, and wind have given me in nourishing those flowers into the beauty that graces my eyes. I only thank the Lord that I am able to look out and feel wholeheartedly the perfect surroundings. How two can be so different and yet so much the same. As I look into the clouds on this sunny day, I can see the beauty of the way they glide so gracefully through the sky, only to see the clouds cover the sun. I watch the sky darken and feel the thrill of anticipation that comes from knowing the clouds will continue on their path and move beyond this place and the sun will shine again.

As you fill space in your house with dried flowers from days gone by, you hold the memory anew in your mind. Looking at these whose moments have passed, you still look forward to the fresh-cut roses to come breathing their fragrance of new life. Deep in your heart out of every flower, tulips would be the one to choose — they come early in the Spring. A sign of the hope the sun has to offer in the midst of the cold winds that surround them, as if they are a blanket that comforts you before the winter has passed.

Some days the clouds gather, darken, and cry, but deep in your heart, know that the beauty of the rain and the rumbling from above will bring forth beautiful flowers which show you love.

Chapter 3

Windows of Life

On the darkest night you can feel so much peace knowing,
looking over the dark shadows of the mountains,
that the sun is soon due to rise again
and chase the shadows away.
You know, deep in your heart,
no matter how dark it may get,
there will always be another sunny day.

A peaceful sun, a sun that is shining
but not as bright because it is at ease.
Knowing the work days before brings
in the beautiful flowers,
that your heart will be pleased.

Looking out of my window I can see so much.
All these things can be complete
with the comfort of a gentle touch.

So take a chance; get out of your seat —
look out your window!
The beauty from above and below has so much to teach.
What God has to offer is further than you
or I alone can reach.

Chapter 4

Windows of Life

The meaning behind this is your windows are your eyes and how you view life. Be careful about the things that you choose to own and know what you need to leave alone.

Flowers represent people. Planting represents home and life, and if you plant someone in your life that means you accept them for whom they are. When you are planting in your life, you're planting for change. When looking out of the window, there are two views.

You can be the person who is planting the flowers and mowing the lawn or you can be the person that has planted the flowers and mowed the lawn. The difference is, the person who is planting is never satisfied with the beauty of what they've planted because they always see more to be done. The person who has planted the flowers and mowed the lawn can look out of the window and enjoy the sun, rain, flowers, moon, stars, and sunrise and know deep in their heart that the beauty they have seen looking out of the window comes from deep within. Knowing that the task is complete, it is time to let what Nature has to offer stand in all its beauty and perfection.

Always trust in God; take time out for yourself to notice the beauty of your surroundings.

By

K. Owens

Alone

Waking up on sleepless nights and I don't know why.

The smallest things that don't matter make me cry. I am reaching out for something and all I feel is air because no one is there.

Alone is how I am feeling.

Alone is something that I face from day to day.

I am so happy and so sad.

Within my family there is so much love and I know exactly where I fit in, but it seems everyone I meet outside my family ends up as just a friend. There are those I could like more, but again it ends up as just friends.

So I guess this is why I am faced with sleepless nights. Walking slowly through the house, searching for something in the kitchen and I realize I am not hungry. I know there is something I am missing, so what am I searching for? I close my eyes and try not to fight sleep, let my mind go blank so that there are no thoughts. It seems as though I have twenty things overlapping in my mind and I am searching for at least one so I can find a little peace.

When facing another day it doesn't matter if it is Monday or the weekend. They are all the same. I start to realize how grateful I am because I hear what everyone else is going through. The good times, the hard times, but most of all they don't have to go through it alone. And I am the sounding board with an ear to listen, a shoulder to cry on, and a few jokes to make you laugh. And I am okay with that because I know my day will come.

I am somebody.

I am not searching because I know I am a great find, but I know I can't be found behind closed doors feeling a little sorrow or lost in my thoughts with nowhere to go.

So I have to make a difference.

I am starting to notice myself in the mirror just a little bit more.

I notice the children's faces when they walk in the room smiling at me as if I said something funny when nothing was said. I love to speak without speaking and laugh just because love exists, traveling silently on an angel's wings, giving each kid just a little giggle. I begin to count the phone calls throughout my day and I finally realize I am somebody and I am not alone. So I will search for happiness to make those silent moments disappear.

If there is silence, it is only me being thankful because I am surrounded by so much love.

Listening to positive music, changing my day-to-day activities just a little bit, surrounding myself with positive people, reading books that inspire me.

I know I am not alone.

I am somebody because I know there is someone who is feeling the same way. I know it is not an easy transitions going from being alone to having somebody. I need to make a change. I can't hold my thoughts and expect my mind to be heard. I must speak out and not hold it in so by the time it needs to come out I am not shouting. Facing myself, getting to know myself so somebody can love me for who I am.

I am not alone and you are not either.

Reach out and if all you feel is air, step into it and breathe it in.

You may just find the one for you.

It might be your best friend or a friend of a friend.

I am somebody.

By K. Owens

It's Over

Facing what could have been…

Facing reality…

It's sad the two cannot co-exist.

Reality is no longer you and I.

What could have been is past tense.

How can I face reality when I thought

what we had was forever?

It's over…

It's over…

How did it come to this?

Even the best picture put together in a puzzle

has its imperfections.

All the little lines represent the challenges in life.

Each shape represents us adapting to each other,

believing in one another, and accepting it

when something doesn't fit.

Having faith in patience

so when the time comes it will fit.

Just in a different place in our lives.

I wanted it to be a perfect puzzle.

When I look back at the puzzle of our lives

I wanted our picture to be so beautiful.

Your eyes wouldn't be able to see the lines

that held our puzzle together

because our love has an essence where

the picture we painted would take your breath away.

Now I am faced with reality…

And I can't breathe…

Because **it's over…**

By K. Owens

Is It Over?

Facing what could have been... Facing reality...

It's sad that those two cannot co-exist.

Reality is no longer you and I.

What could have been is past tense.

How can I face reality when I thought

what we had was heaven sent?

Is it over? Is it over?

How did it come to this?

Even the best picture put together in a puzzle

has it's own imperfections.

All the little lines represent the challenges in life.

Each shape represents us adapting to each other,

believing in one another, and accepting it

when something doesn't fit.

Having faith in patience so when the time comes it will fit.

Just in a different place in our lives.

I wanted it to be a perfect puzzle.

When I look back at the puzzle of our lives

I wanted our picture to be so beautiful.

Your eyes wouldn't be able to see the lines that held our puzzle

together because our love has such an essence where

a picture that we painted would take your breath away.

Here is a gift ...

Before we say goodbye

We both know we put our puzzle together too quickly.

Let's talk and take the time to see if we can start over.

As the box is being opened it slowly reveals

a picture of the two of them.

Inside, the picture is in a thousand pieces.

They sit down with tears in their eyes

because they realize the magnitude of the love

they almost lost over something so simple.

They sit down and begin putting the puzzle together,

Choosing each piece patiently.

It's not over because our past and our present

can co-exist because we still exist.

I love you and I love you too.

By
K. Owens

Everything is Fine

Today for some reason I felt like crying inside when there is nothing wrong with today. I just want to ball up into a knot and feel the chills all over my body and it's 90 degrees. I want to cry and I want to push the tears from my eyes searching for more tears. I don't know why. There is nothing really wrong. I didn't hear a sad song and wasn't faced with any challenges—I'm just feeling sadness inside.

Grabbing as many pillows as I can, just because I can. The phone is ringing and I don't want to answer so I don't. There's a knock on the door and I don't answer because I won't. Why do I want to cry when there's no reason for me to cry? I cry anyway. Nothing I have looks good. I don't like the way my face looks or my skin. My clothes seem as if they are all faded and outdated when some still have the tags on them. Wiping away the tears because there is something that I fear and I don't know what it is.

There's nothing wrong with today. Looking outside, everything seems so peaceful. I can feel inside that there's a perfect storm. My heart is racing as if it's in a race for it's life. My lungs are filled with air and it seems as if I can't push it out. My mind is blank so I don't have what it takes to figure it out. I feel like I'm falling and I know I'm just laying here on the bed. I want to open my eyes but I'm just a little too afraid. I can feel the sunlight. There's no reason for me to feel this way because yesterday was fine. The day before, I finally got those shoes I've always wanted and last night when I laid down to go to bed, the last thing I said is I love you to someone I care about, but when I woke up, this is how I felt even though everything is fine.

By
K. Owens

Faith

Trust and believe in yourself.

Smile every chance you get.

Your life is in your hands, so reach out,

and if you fall,

spread your wings, because it's time to fly.

Faith
K. Owens

Thoughts of you

You left this morning on your way to work and I was still asleep yet falling in love with you all over again. Just hearing the sounds of your feet walking around trying to get ready, I was caught in between the worlds of being awake and sound asleep. I can hear your blow dryer and I fell deeper into sleep. When I heard the water running I eased up a little closer to being awake and the sounds of little things being moved around. I felt peace within the sheets. When I heard the door shut and I woke up, just lying there thinking how could I be so blessed?

As I wobble into the bathroom I can smell your perfume and I get lost in a daze and I see all the things plugged in all over the counter. Even though my eyes are halfway shut my heart is beating just to keep up. This made me love you even more. When I sit down on the bed pondering, lying down again, I give a silent moment, being thankful that you are my best friend. I realize I am saying it out loud, talking to the heavens...... Slowly as I get ready. I notice how your clothes are hung just a little differently than mine and mine are hung differently than what I would have done on my own. So I have changed. I wonder, if someone could see the grin I have on my face would they say, "That is amazing". By the time I think about what time it is, it is time to go. I look back just for a second and my thoughts are.... I will never let you go.

Sitting in my car waiting for it to get warm when I am warm inside. I never felt a tears on my cheek when I wasn't sad and now I feel it. I understand that they are tears of joy. Before I even get to work I call you three times. Even though you told me you were going to be in a meeting I call anyway with hopes that your meeting was cancelled or perhaps you are just passing by your desk. It's funny how love sometimes makes you forget everything you were told the day before and I realize why that is...... Because you are not keeping score, you are letting your heart soar and you surrender to the now.

How do I know? This is how. I love you.

Thoughts of you.

By

K. Owens

Love

Love is first finding yourself from within
in order to love someone else.
Chasing the words, what people call love,
you will always be a day late and a dollar short.
Love is surrounding yourself for what is to be and what is not.
Understanding love is not trying to please.
Love is a tingle in your fingertips. Love is
that feeling you feel in your knees.
Love is something that you chase even
if you know that there's no game.
Love is taking a deep breath and being able to laugh
and cry at the same time.
Love is for what gain?
Love is something you see with your eyes closed
and are willing to accept whatever comes first.
First, second, or last.
I know love is something that you get from above
that gives you reason
to want to pray for happiness forever and a day.
So in order to be complete,
the only way you can find the love
that you seek is through Christ.

To sum it up...there's not one word that explains love.

You don't have to chase love, you just slow down

and face it and then accept it.

Love is something that you run with from within.

And if you feel like you can fly, spread your arms,

and catch the wind.

Then you know it's from within.

When we get to heaven we will ask, what is that one word??

Then and only then, it shall be spoken. Now it is written...

Love

By
K. Owens

Monday through Sunday

Today I smiled about yesterday
because yesterday was about us.
Tomorrow is about our future.
My sun shines just as bright at night
as it does during the day.
Because you made my yesterday something
I never want to throw away.
I know I will see you forever and a day.
I live yesterday, and today it will be done the right way.
I'm not afraid to think about yesterday or last week.
I'm humble with joy because we have each other
Monday through Sunday.
Seems as if it's one day.
Because we found the secret that there is no yesterday
without tomorrow to follow.
There is no sunset without the moon to follow.
So our days will stay the same;
it's up to us to make the change.

K. Owens

Trust

What we have is our trust

We don't have to put that in writing.

We have to put it in trust.

Be true from within

You shall find your lifelong friend.

Soul Mates Forever.

By
K. Owens

MLK

Today was kind of a crazy day. Trying to figure out what's up, what's down, and somehow it seems as if I'm going in circles. All of a sudden I heard a speech that was called "I Have a Dream." It was coming through the speakers of my computer, and my mom and my friend were just listening. I sat there on the couch just for a moment because the words were so powerful. Getting chills all over my body, trying to fight back tears and not knowing why. Oh such a wonderful dream.

If only we could live that dream then life would be such a dream that you could live. People coming together to change…knowing that our purpose is to get along and see each other as the same. There are so many different races, and we forget in each race there are different faces. We all are not the same in some ways because we don't look alike. People point a finger and think you're wrong because you're not the same as them. They fail to look next to them to the person that is the same color and they don't look like you. Same color, different face…it's all about love; it's not about race. This dream that is a dream that is coming through these speakers makes me want to run out and knock on each door and tell everyone to come outside just so we can see the purpose of life. Everyone in the same neighborhood having the same purpose. Just to come outside. You only see it on TV — why can't we see that in reality? People come home nowadays. Technology has changed the way we view each other. Now instead of getting out of your car and having a chance to wave to your neighbors, you can push a button and your garage opens and before you know it it's closed. In just an instant, we miss opportunities of saying "hi" and "hello" and "how are you?" It gives us distance.

He had a dream. His dream is more powerful than any dream or should I say most dreams. That dream shouldn't be a dream; it should be reality because we can sit at the same table, we can hold hands, we all can bow our heads and say the same prayer in different voices and also in different languages. Even though we don't understand each other and/or language is different, the fact that we can stand before each other says that we are the same and we can make a difference. If the man that wrote this dream who said that I have a dream could see us now, he would be so happy that we came so far but so sad that we are so blind because we're falling apart.

What is your dream? We all can have a dream, and the greatest thing about a dream is that you can have so many different illusions and so many different ways that you want life to be. The things that are not possible you can leave within your sleep. Those that can be made possible, you can chase as soon as you're awake. You can't change the world alone, but you can change your world when you realize you are not alone. Instead of speaking out loud, say it on the inside. Let your actions of goodness and your graceful footsteps get you to your resting place. Be humble and powerful enough to move trees. Now that would be a dream, and if that's not your dream, what is your dream? MLK.

By

K. Owens

Oh Say Can We See

Oh say can we see these soldiers who are fighting for you and me? Precious time we take for granted when each moment they're dodging elements and situations just to save their own lives so they can have more time to save ours.

Oh say can we see the soldiers who are fighting for you and me? Have we taken each minute for granted? Five minutes pass by and sometimes we can't remember what happened three minutes ago. The soldiers are fighting for the precious minutes that we have and they can just about tell you about every second that has passed. They're counting the ones to come.

So intense, on alert, mind and body is not the same because of their loved ones who are fighting next to them. Some are hurt, hoping and praying that today will not be their day. Some of us get up in the morning and the night comes so quick. This is something we have to think about. Oh say can we see each and every soldier who has lost their lives fighting for precious seconds that we take for granted? At their last moments if they can see what we see, would it be worth them risking their lives so we can be?

People get angry because someone cuts them off driving down the street when there's a soldier who can't sleep because one of their fellow soldiers just died in a Humvee. They're just a little confused about what they're fighting for. As the minutes pass their families are on edge and can't sleep. They're hoping that their child, sister, or brother comes home next week.

Sometimes if you cut someone off because you're driving, before you give a finger to a stranger just think — the person who just cut you off could've been lost in a daze thinking about the days when they had their sister, their brother, husband, or wife by their side. They couldn't see you because it was just a little blurry in the mirror from the lost tears they're trying to fight back just so they can make it throughout the day.

Oh say can we see the soldiers within you and me? We can fight for them while they're fighting for us. You could pay attention more to a school bus, a motorcycle or someone lost in a daze thinking back. Or someone full of tears for what they have lost. It's not about what we see and it's not about what we feel…it's reality. That's real.

You can feel a certain way and someone can be completely different. If you're humble you understand the precious moments to be sitting at a light and waiting for it to turn green or being able to order your food and sit at a table. Within those precious minutes, someone fighting for you has become disabled. They lost a limb or they lost a life. Husband and wife, kids searching for a new way to live .Oh say can we change and rearrange so we all can come together and face the pain and smile at the person who is flipping you off? Slow down for the person who is trying to get by. Turn your radio down sometimes just so you can cry because someone has died for you and me.

Oh say can you see the soldiers who have fought and died for you and me?

Oh say can you see?

By
K. Owens

Family

Where are you? Where have you been? Back in the days family was more important than friends. Family was friends but friends meant that you were family. So where are you? Upset because someone has something newer than what you have. Can't get along with someone and don't know why. When a question is asked, you have something negative to say. So what happened to family? We all have forgotten that family is the greatest word that has ever been spoken besides love, and somehow we've lost it in the midst of falling in love with someone who is not family.

Sometimes we fall in love with someone who wants us for our physical, spiritual, or financial selves, and all other reasons but who knows where we've gotten lost. I guess it really doesn't matter where we made the wrong turn, what does matter is finding our way back to start all over again. When you came into this world the most important people to you were the family that you believed in...

There was a time when you wanted to see your family and it just couldn't wait. Because the love that you had for family was so deep, it was just fate. You loved it for no reason, you chased it with everything you had to chase with and you still chased it even if you knew you couldn't catch it.

Family now consists mostly of the neighborhood that you live in versus the family that you were born within. There are families that are keeping the true tradition of what families are supposed to be like. Don't forget to love the people that you share the same blood with and to love the people that you don't. I see families from state to state, and they find reasons not to see each other over the cost of a steak. You have a year to prepare for a family reunion but you've put rims on your car and bought a new sofa and now those reason are why you can't make it.

What is family? Family is something that you are be able to see through the blurriness of a tear because it means so much. Family is something that you feel right now through your whole body tingling just from that simple touch from someone that you love. A voice that you haven't heard from in such a long time. Kids are being born in this world when you have no idea who the father or mother is, and the most important thing are our own kids, and sometimes that doesn't matter at all. We're thinking about that picture that we want to buy or what we can afford to hang on that wall.

Where is family? For some reason a child grows up amongst a family and family is all that they believe in and every family member is a true friend. Everyone is going in different directions and searching for something once they get above age and they forget about that place that they lived in, cried in, crawled on, and slept on, and the only thing that matters is what they can step on to get to the next level. Come on, that's not family. If you're stepping on something, with family, you're stepping on the hands of the people who are lifting you to a higher level so you can reach down to pull them up. You don't look down and complain about the one's fingertips that weren't touching the shoe that pushed you up to where you are, to who you are today. You reached down because they were a part of who you are today. That's family.

Family is something that you surf on when there's no water. Family is the greatest musical that can ever be heard when there's no music. Family is a perfect waterfall trickling down through all the rocks, leading down to a perfect stream, and it's not a dream, it's reality. That's family.

Let's stop hating and faking the relationships that we have amongst each other. Let's stop fighting and having jealousy and anger amongst sisters and brothers, cousins, uncles and aunties, grandmas and grandpas. We can't forget the way it was. Every day somebody's life changes; every step something is rearranged.

I see people eating in neighbor's homes and having the greatest barbeques, but in reality no one at that barbeque knows you. They know you for who you are today and what you left behind, but they don't know that person that had their head down thinking about how life used to be and how it could be. Right now there's somebody that you don't get along with. If you really ask the question why you don't, you really don't have an answer. Because if it's something that they did or something that they said, you've got to think about it — you did something and you said something, too. You're not perfect either.

Everyone has to grow, and in order to grow you have to reach out for life, so there has to be change; but we can't look at each other as if in the change that we're making, we're not the same. We all have to adapt to our own environment, because we have a different route to heaven and a different journey. That's what makes family and friends so important. Because you can bring so many different stories that bring a great book together and can be a legacy that is read throughout the years, people can cry about all the tears. We can laugh about all the happy times and we can search for the things we had to find but we remain together because we are family.

A family reunion is meant for people to come together and talk about their state, how they've done with life, what has changed. I'm not better than you, you're not better than me, but this is what I see within my family. That's family. Everyone driving up in different cars from different states and countries. That is the greatest thing. It doesn't matter the emblem or the sign that is on the side of that car, the only thing that matters is the heart and the commitment that it took to pay for that car. The home you live in, whether it's a mansion or it's something that is so small that you just barely turn around in, truly in your heart you should always have a great friend that sees you for whom you are.

We are all fortunate in different ways. Someone might be fortunate to have a house with ten thousand square feet with less of a heart. Someone can be modest and grateful for a house that they can barely turn around in. So appreciate what you have without comparing to someone else's, because in God's eyes we're all the same.

Take the gift that you have and show your gift to the people that you love. Help them achieve things that you have achieved. So roll up your sleeves because it's time to work for each other. Pick up a shovel, pick up a hammer...help those who are willing to work for what they want and teach them how to build what you have, so we can all have the same. That is family.

Family- you can walk in the room and smell so many different perfumes, so many different colognes, but it doesn't matter who wears what because it is home. That's family.

You should be running to a family reunion, you should be walking to a family reunion. Flying and crying because of a family reunion... you need to be there. Because even as we speak and you're reading this, someone is dying. They might not know it, or even if they do know it, it's time for you to show that your love is for real and your love is for the hereafter not just for now. You're no different than the person that stands before you. You are you, they are they, and that is what makes our day, our day, because we are family. Love one another.

No matter how much you have to search, no matter what you had to find, you hold onto your family because that is what you hold on to when you are swinging through the jungle of everything to try to make you forget what family is.

Family reunion, hello, goodbye, hello, goodbye. Family reunion. You say hello to the ones you love; you say goodbye to the ones you adore. You loved and adored them when they came through the door. That is your family and you are family. You're just as important as anyone who came who is a part of your family. And if there is someone who passed by outside on the street and wasn't a part of the same blood and the love — they are still the same from the One up above so you all are still family. You think about that.

Family
K. Owens

I Love You

I love you for no reason and even reason has no reason
but the love is there.
I love you just because and when I think about because...
there's no answer.
I love you for just the sound of the word.
I love to love when I love you.
Every day when I think about the word love,
I'm chasing a dream. I'm chasing reality.
I'm chasing something that's within me
that I've never been able to find,
I've just been able to feel.
I can feel it in my toes. I feel it in my elbows, my knees.
I feel it in my throat.
My mind, when I see life it's just not the same.
I walk differently just because. I love differently just because.
I love you because I've never been able to find a flower
that represents the love that I have for you.
I find myself searching for flowers to show the love
that I have for you.
I just want to say that I love you.
I love you for the silent moments
that I have when I'm thinking about love.
I love you for love.
When there are hard times in my life and I think about love,
those times are not as difficult.
So I'm saying, **I love you.**
Lying in the bed silent amongst the sheets. Looking at the
ceiling lost in a daze.
Thinking about all the ways that I can love and all the
differences of love.

Knowing that I'm lost in love.
So I'm saying, I love you.
I want to reach out my hand, open up my heart.
Show the world my soul, my spirit.
You help me feel the feeling
that I have within my heart to get near it.
Searching to the heavens for a word that is more potent
than the word love,
because when I say love it just doesn't seem like
that word can represent how I feel.
It seems as if there can be a greater
than greater word that can be said.
That can be heard throughout the valley.
I wonder what that word is.
But until then, the only words
that I have are — **I love you.**
I love you for you, I love you for me, **I love you for us.**
I love you for the patience
that I have when I love you, knowing that there's no rush.
So all I'm saying is...**I love you.**

I Love You
K. Owens

Our Lives

My life, my life, your life, your life, our lives.

What are we going to do to change it? What are we going to do to change it?

So we don't have to go through the same cycle over and over again.

The change has to be made and it has to be made today, right now.

So what are we going to do?

Are we finally going to be able to ride down the street and get cut off and show no emotions? What are we going to do about it?

Can we look at our friends' and our families' faces and say that we are true? Can we? We can't change the whole world, but we can change our world. The world exists around us individually.

Every person sees the world differently than the person next to them.

No matter if you were raised in the same home, lying next to someone, you still feel alone. Someone can drop a cup of water, and one person can think; how can you do that? The next person can think of a solution, instantly running to the bathroom to get a towel. What are we going to do? Let's stop living our lives for statistics, because statistics are what's killing us. Because everybody thinks the way they think is the best way to think. There's nothing wrong with the way you think, but you have to have room for compromise. That's what life is all about.

My life, your life, our lives. Not just your opinion...his opinion, her opinion, and our opinions. Just accepting an opinion with the option for another opinion and being able to put it together. Who's right? Who's wrong? We both could be right, we both could be wrong; but the right thing about it is whether you're right or wrong you both are willing to accept the other person's opinion.

Our lives have to change. We have to be able to walk down the street and wave at our neighbors. It's just not our arm saying hi; it's the heart and soul. Finding ourselves being fake at times when someone says, "Hey, how you doin'?" You find yourself saying, "Hey, how you doin'?" in the same tone. Find our tone, follow your path, be yourself. That's what our lives are all about. It's not about everyone else's opinion. Let's live it, let's change it.

It's funny, when the phone rings everyone has a different ring tone. Everybody has a different ring tone, and on some occasions you hear someone have the same ring tone as yours. Does that mean that they share the same views that you do? I don't think so. So accepting someone for who they are is first accepting you, and trusting that you can be you, not having to change just because someone else is different, as well as not having an opinion just because they are different or their opinion about you is the same.

Different cultures; we all have different things that we do. It's not racism, but there are different things that each culture does. Some things. It doesn't make you different, it makes you — you. Difference is a difference that shows difference, and it gives us miles and miles to learn about the difference so somehow we can change within ourselves to understand differences so we can be different but also the same. So we learn not to judge, we learn how to love. Reach out your hand and shake somebody's hand. Can you feel the grip? Or is there no grip? Does that mean that person is more confident than the other? Statistics. Shake somebody's hand. It doesn't matter how they shake yours. Shake it because it's a man, a woman, it's a boy, a child. Because if that child is three and you're sixty, you both are equal at shaking hands. So it's not about the grips; it's about the heart and the time spent. So let's shake hands.

Going to the grocery store. So many things to buy. Passing people with different things in their basket. Some people are healthier than the others. Doesn't make you any better. There are people who eat healthy every day that die every day. People who eat badly every day, die every day. Life is more about how you see it and how you want to preserve it. Do what you do that makes you — you. Don't change who you are and your opinion because we do what we do. What makes us — us.

We never know when our day is to come. Let's enjoy our steps and the space that we feel while we're in it. One person could be eating a cheesecake while the other could be eating a steak. The one with the steak can get hit by a car. We don't wish that on anybody. Years and tears. We all have to face our fears and that's death. So our time is precious. Let's take it for what it is. Let thee, Let thee.

What you see before you. Chase the goals that were in your heart and help the ones who are chasing theirs by being confident in the ones you have. When you talk about your achievements, talk about them, as the things that you accomplished an in such a way that you are not putting down someone else who didn't accomplish the same goals. Their goals could be different and they accomplish them the same way, but in your eyes you don't measure up the same way. We all know eyes that are wide open can be more blind than the eyes that see and the eyes that can't see. You, me, us...let's change the way we live. Each individual person, we all have our own route, our own footsteps. Our own way of wearing our clothes and tying our shoes. Our own thoughts and option to choose.

That is life...Accept it, live freely...
Your life is in your hands.

K. Owens

Have You Ever?

Have you ever thought about crying for no reason? Have you ever thought about wanting to pick up the phone and call someone for no reason? Have you ever let a day go past and forgot to pray when you know you needed to pray? Have you ever?

Have you ever thought of love, ever thought of love in a way that love should be within you and wondered if someone felt the same way that you do? Have you ever?

Have you ever sat inside your home and watched TV and heard it rain so hard outside and wondered why? Have you ever seen the lightning just shining and wondering how many lives have changed just in a split second? Have you ever?

Have you ever thought about life in a way where you're not selfish? Where you are willing to learn so much about others and not have a real reason why, but the reason why is the reason why you started to cry, and didn't know why? Sometimes that could be just because missing love from different views. Sometimes not finding it, you have so much to lose. We all are different and we all are so much the same. That's the reason why we all share the same pain.

Have you ever been driving in your car singing a song knowing in your heart you don't sound anywhere like the song sounds, but you sing it anyway? Because that is your way to sing that song. It makes you feel like you. Have you ever?

Have you ever thought about a family member, friend, loved one, or a lost love and didn't pick up the phone when you know you have everything within you to do it, but you just couldn't find the words to see through it? Have you ever?

Now is the time, even when you can't find the words...you pick up the phone anyway. And even if there are no words, your phone call is just enough. Can you ever? Can you ever take a step past a step that you never thought you would ever take to change the fate of your life? Have you ever? And if you haven't, you should.

Have you ever thought about all the moments that it took just for you to learn how to learn to feel the pain and become stronger so it's not the same? Have you ever?

Have you ever been lost for words and didn't know what to say? Didn't know how to face the day, didn't know how you got up? You didn't know, you just didn't know. Have you ever?

Have you ever wanted to change your life and wanted to wait until tomorrow or next week just to change it? Well, by the time tomorrow comes and next week has passed you lost so much. Have you ever? The minute that you think of tomorrow and next week is the minute that you need to start preparing for tomorrow or next week. When tomorrow comes your journey begins. So when next week comes, your journey has been walked on. So by the time you think of it again, it has passed and you've grown from it. Have you ever? And if you haven't, you should.

You're not alone in this world. Just because you feel alone doesn't mean that you are alone. When you see someone else and you see they're somewhat the same as you...arms, feet, heart and soul, spirit...you should truly believe because you are truly near it. Reach out for what you believe in. Let's stop saying, "Have you ever" and instead say, "We have. So this is life.

Have You Ever

K. Owens

Crazy Love

Can you hear that music? The beat sounds so deep

Can you hear it?

You can't?

What is that sound?

Can you hear it?

You can't?

Why is my voice changing?

I feel like I walk differently for some reason and it always sounds like music or something. I have been trying to figure it out but at the same time I am O.K. with it. I really don't understand it but it feels good.

Can you hear that?

You can't.

How come I can hear it and you can't?

      You don't know?

Do I act differently?

      I do?

Huh?

My smile is bigger?

I didn't notice that.

And why is everything funny?

I don't know, it just is sometimes.

Can you hear that music? It sounds like a feeling because I can't explain the words?

No?

Well I will talk to you later. I got to get home. I know there is something different about me because I am riding in the car with no music and singing words to a song that is probably being written as I speak.

My friends say I have changed but in a good way and I wonder what way that is?

Is it because of where I am headed or that I am not alone?

Am I crazy to be thinking this way when no one is in here but me?

People riding next to me must think something is funny because I just feel so happy sometimes getting lost in a daze. When I went to the mall to get something for me and I realized I end up shopping for someone else.

Slowly I realize it is because I have fallen in love. I can miss and reminisce and be happy about this at the same time. I can hear a beat and it is coming through my chest so now I can rest because I am not alone.

Can you hear that?

I think I can because now I know what it is and now my phone is ringing and my heart is singing.

Hi honey. No I am on the way home.

Hey, I have a question to ask you. Do you notice something different with me?

Hmmm....you do?

Sometimes when you are alone can you hear music?

You can?

Hmmm.... Do you know what the song is?

Not really but you kinda do?

Well I am here to tell you I found out what that song is.

No, I am going to wait until I get home to tell you.

O.K. O.K. I will tell you now.

It is called US.

No the song is called Usssssss!!!

Because your heart is beating and mine is beating and we can
hear it. We smile differently because of each other and we can
feel it. My heart is not heavy. It is so light and it feels right.

Are you serious?

So it is not just me?

I thought I was going crazy?

Now I know we are crazy for each other and crazy in love.

Crazy in Love.

By
K. Owens

On My Way Home from Work

I'm on my way home from work stressing about everything I had to go through just for work. But it's the end of the day and I'm happy about that. It's so weird because I have to go and find another family through work in order to make it right at home. Walking in my home, turning on the lights. There is a TV, and if there isn't a TV there's a TV in the plans. Having to get up every morning to go and do something whether I love it or not, but one way or another it's done just because I have to have a reason to want to be someone. There's no way I can make it in this world without having some kind of finances in order to makes ends meet. Somebody has to work for somebody so you can take care of somebody even if that somebody is just you and your family. Somebody has to be taken care of.

Most jobs are not the best jobs. Some jobs are the best jobs. One way or another, it's still a job. Something that we have to do just so we can take care of ourselves Sometimes, I ask why life has to be this way. Why is it we have to face another day to make a way just to have a day. Spending eight to ten to fourteen hours at work. It doesn't matter the hours, we just can't wait to get home to take a shower and to relax for the time that we do have. Sometimes we can't even do that because we have so many things to take care of that we couldn't take care of throughout our day. Everything has to be planned. Every situation is different. Lunch — we only have so many minutes. It's sad, but that's just the way that it is.

Some people are fortunate to not have to work because they are born within wealth. In some ways they still have to work for what they have because they have to deal with the life of having money so it becomes work on it's own. So why is it? How come we all have to work for somebody? Why do we have to do something to make ends meet? Why is life so hard to the point where we can't just get up and spend our lives every day just loving one another? There has to be a change in our lives to make us rearrange our lives. Then there comes problems because we're so stressed for the things that we have to do just to make our lives become easier.

Six o'clock in the morning the alarm clock rings. It's time to get up. Some people have to get up at six, seven, eight, or nine. Some in the mornings, some in the evenings. But either way it's something that we all have to achieve in order for us to have shoes, clothes, and to be able to have buttons that we have on our sleeves. So what do we have to do to change that? Because that's a way of life. The evil of money has changed so many lives because we have to give up so many hours of our lives so we can live. It just doesn't seem fair. Because no one cares for the time that we spend to make what we have. They only care about what was done within the time that we had to make what we have, which is sad.

I'm here to tell you that your worth is more than a dollar. Your worth is more than the hour that you spend typing on that computer, cutting hair, bouncing that basketball, serving food or working in a warehouse. Driving a truck delivering furniture. It doesn't matter what you do because, whatever it is, you're better than that. So you have to find some kind of happiness even with those things that you have to do to make ends meet, those changes you make to make a better life. You have someone working on the cash register that doesn't want to be there. Sometimes they really don't have anything to share with you while they are there. They are looking at the clock because it's time for them to go home, and if it's not time for them to go home, they wish it was. Playing sports, being so competitive, it's got to get to you at some times. There are so many teams, and only one person can win in the end. So the whole year all the struggles and all the training to get you there just wasn't enough because someone else won. Don't hold your head down, be proud that you are part of the game and you have already won just by stepping onto the field.

Your worth is more important than any game or any challenge. Look into the eyes of the ones who love you and you will see a glimpse of your true worth. We have to realize the love, hugs, laughter and joy, and heaven that is above, is more precious than the money that we have that controls us. In some way, no matter what we say and how we say it...money has something to do with the happiness that we do have because when there is none, there's nothing there to feed the young.

Heavenly Father, help us become a nation of people that is humble to joy and laughter and the wholeheartedness of joy and live to have life so we can be happy throughout these times and things that we have to face just to live. Please give us the strength to be able to be us and face ourselves amongst all the ups and downs of life so we can have life to live life. There is a way for us all to make a way. Just give us that spirit and that drive and that insight to see it and believe it. Control it so we can be it. So we can accept it in our heart and soul so therefore we can see it. So we can see the guidelines of life, which we should travel instead of being confused with all the things that have us battered and abused. Give us the insight to be humble and walk amongst the sharp rocks with soft feet; to fly amongst the valleys, to feel the wind; to walk within the darkness and feel the light inside; and only search for the things that we know that are good for us. Give us the strength to overcome our trials and tribulations and have the will to stand up and fight for what we believe in.

In the Lord, Jesus Christ's name we pray.

Amen.

On My Way Home From Work
K. Owens

Good Morning

Good morning to you. Getting up slowly, barely can open my eyes glancing down at the pillow, seeing that it's all beat up and crunched like it just got out of a heavyweight fight.

Walking away, looking back, realizing every dent that's in that pillow was just me through the night fighting for life.

Noticing the way the sheets and the blanket have been shifted around as if I was fighting for the path by pushing things away just so my feet can touch the ground. I can feel my blessing through the chill in the floor while glancing over seeing my shoes tucked away in the closet.

Being able to hear birds outside the window. It sounds like four maybe five...I don't know but it's a perfect harmony because I can feel myself lost in darkness all night and now I can taste the light. I have the will to fight.

Once again it starts. It's a good morning to have a morning of stretching my arms, being able to yawn and cracking my back.

Getting out of bed, wobbling to the bathroom, one eye open barely, the other eye closed. Just being able to process the light that is coming through the blinds. It's just a little too much for me to look dead on. So I take what I can and squint my eyes.

The bathroom is a place that I can wash this sleep off my face.

Walking like a little kid, wobbling from leg to leg. It's like a gentle giant. No matter how old or young you are, you're walking like a gentle giant.

Knees, arms, and elbows working together to help us get this body together to fight that weather that's outside.

The sun, the rain, the snow...who knows, but at this time, it's time for me to put on my clothes.

Thankful to even have clothes.

Wishing and hoping that today is a better day than yesterday regardless of how yesterday was. Yesterday could've been great...

Some had sad days but today we pray for better days so it's good morning.

Good morning, stretch my arms and yawning. Fighting to get through so I can see it through. Today is the day that I can face my fate.

I can work, I can deal with the hurt and pain, smile for the joy. It's a great day.

It's a good morning.

Walking out of the bathroom noticing everything that I notice before realizing there was a big battle in that bed the way the bed is all crumpled up. I smile for happiness because God brought me through it.

I didn't know when I tossed and turned. I can't remember how the blankets got so messed up.

Looking into the corner, seeing the pillow three feet from the bed.

I don't remember how that pillow got over there that far.

Maybe through my fighting and through the struggles of life at night. A past that I've been pulled through to see my fate but it was the pillow that was over my face and an angel helped me get it away. That's life. That's love.

So it's a good morning, stretching my arms while I'm yawning. I'm awake now, eyes both wide open, still barely can process the light but I'm thankful to have life because it is a good morning.

Good Morning
K. Owens

Smile

Nate and Wendy

How do we even begin to tell you what you both mean to us?
You've been through a lot over the last few months; we can feel
the weight of the smiles that you have on your faces from time to
time, no matter how heavy the weight of your smile is,
you smile anyway.
So how do we begin to tell you what you mean to us?
I guess a start is to smile back.
Here's a little something to show you what we see in you.
From your reflection in your eyes no matter what you go through
we know you see it in us.
A flower can be the most beautiful thing the eyes can see,
but it's more beautiful when we see your smiles smiling back at us.
A night on the town just for you two
and all of us in the neighborhood will hold back the hands of time
so you can have more time to say to each other,
"I love you."
Your spirit and your example is the way families should be.
It helps give us all a reason to want to be.
No matter what you go through in life, it's a **blessing** to have life.

Wendy

Your husband **loves** you more than the anticipation of another day.
When I see the mountains they are so beautiful.
When I see his face looking at you,
I can see a glimmer of the mountains from his
eyes in the way he is looking at you.
I have never seen anything as **beautiful** as that.
His eyes are glazed over holding back tears that he wants to shed,
but he doesn't shed them because he's being **strong** for you.

Nate

Your wife is the *queen* of all queens.
A mother and a wife to be *proud* of.
Her *inspiration*, her *drive*, her *will* to never give up
being the *best* that she is.
You can feel that *real love* just the way she embraces
her kids, her family, and friends.
Smile.

So we're smiling for you, because when times get hard
we know you're all smiling for us.
Let's smile together.

Take another glance at the flowers throughout the
neighborhood and know deep in your heart that no
matter how *beautiful* those flowers are,
It doesn't compare to the air that we share because we're
breathing with you.
We're *grateful* for that.
We all can come together and walk out of our homes and
hold hands.
We can share a prayer while breathing the same air.
We're *thankful* to be a part of your lives.

Let's smile together, let's come together and we can
weather any storm,
because there's always an arm and a shoulder to lean on.
Take a day to just be with one another and we all will hold
back the hands of time.
That way you can have more time to see and feel what's
real within the minutes and the seconds while you're
riding together and holding hands and sitting down to eat
with one another.

On the way home if you can feel the chills,
it's the prayers from all the butterflies we've sent out to
protect you.
And when you don't feel every little bump in the street,
it's the prayers from the neighborhood making your
weight just a little lighter.
We'll see you, because it's time to come home and when
you're not in the neighborhood, home just doesn't feel like
home.
(Get Well Soon.)

Smile
K. Owens

Solutions Instead of Excuses

Excuses are riding down the street with rims on our car, tint on the windows, cell phone in our hand being less than a man when there's a child going without and you know who you are. I can say that because I was one of you. The solution to the priority of life is more important than anything that is materialistic. It's more important than the club, the latest CD. We have to stop playing the victim when there's someone else that is a victim.

We would think if we went through it and knew how hard it was... why do we continue to do it to a child who is searching for that lost love? Where's my father? Where's my mother? I'm sad because the guilt is killing me. I'm asking heaven, please, I don't want to live my life without because I have lived without. I don't know how to be a father, but who does? Each person standing in their shoes, I'm quite sure they doubt something. That doesn't give us a reason to run from it. I'm going to take a stand today to be the man that I'm supposed to be, but I don't have the words for the silence, the missed days of going to the school, buying those shoes and clothes to help them get through. I have no excuses for that, and I know I have to pay for that.

Sometimes I wonder why everything doesn't go my way, and in some ways I know why my days are the way that they are. I am going to work on that to become better. You should too. We should never brag on something that we are supposed to do. When it's your day to spend with your child...it's not babysitting. Let's get over that. You're not babysitting; you're spending time with your child! It should be a privilege for you. At the time when that person is picking up that child you should be asking when is the next day that I get him or her or them. Because we forget that we were once a child at some time and no one needs to pay for what we went through. Whether your life was great or whether it was bad... each kid deserves to have a mother in their life and even a dad. I can tell my son that I'm sorry, but it doesn't make up for those past years and the tears that he shed or hearing my voice on the phone and being misled. But I won't make that mistake anymore. Bought my plane ticket yesterday and I know that doesn't make up for lost time. There's nothing great about the choice that I just made because it's something that I'm supposed to do so there is no praise. I guess it's all about us being real no matter what it is in your life that you're going without.

For all the times when you're laughing like you have the world in your hands and you're in control, your youth will only be your youth for a certain time. You have to face the days for when you get old, if you make it there. So your life is not just about your life, it's our lives, his life, her life, and their lives. We can make a change. Let's not just pick up the phone...Let's do something right. Most people in this world can understand what you are doing and what you have done more than they can deal with what you've said. So what is your excuse? There's a solution to every problem. I am working on my solution. It doesn't make me great by any means, but I am working on my solution. You should too. Change and rearrange everything in your life because their life is more important than just your life. Saying I'm sorry is not good enough. Making a change shouldn't be that tough.

Turned on the TV today; a kid is missing. A child has come up missing. School is calling, complaining because a kid is not listening. Too young to understand why there's not a man or a woman that is supposed to be there. I can't wait 'til the day when all of the fathers and mothers that had excuses can have their own parade with their kids and call it the parade of solutions. Coming together to change things, to make things right. Making things right is making it today, because no one can make up for yesterday and the years past. The solution is making a stand. Calling when you say you were going to call, showing up when you are supposed to. Listening when you need to. Being what you are supposed to be. Even though at times when it hurts you to go through because the time that you have missed. As long as you have life you have time to give life and to show life.

So let's find our solutions. Let's make our parade. Let's step up to the microphone and tell the world about our stories of how we made it. How we changed it. We can slow down the numbers of kids that are going to prison. We can lift up the grades for the kids who are daydreaming in class thinking about lost time or how they're going to find the person that is missing. A start is a start no matter where the start is. If you read this today and can't make a change today then your day has not started because this is real. Everyone can change. So there has to be a solution. So let's find it. Let's get that parade. I miss you son. I'll see you soon. From a father who didn't know how to be a father who didn't have a father. So pray for us.

Solutions Instead of Excuses
K. Owens

It's Time to grow up

The other day someone asked me what made me change? Instantly I said when my son was born because when he came into this world I was still a child at heart. He taught me how to be a father by reaching out and crying for me and then the father in me had to face the boy in me and teach him the greatest lesson ever learned; how to be a man.

It's Time to Grow up.

By
K. Owens

Silence

Silence. There's not even a whisper.
And there is a thought but it's still **silence**
because the thought hasn't been thought
of enough to bring to life.
Being alone, standing amongst people
with laughter and smiling...
but there's still **silence**.
Silence from myself and everyone else...
finding peace from within.
Just being able to look at people and read their lips,
what they have to say. **Silence**...being able to hear a
waterfall when there is no waterfall
There is silence because it's only a thought.
Thinking of how to make a better way
for tomorrow and it's **silence,**
because there's no one to talk to.
Being alone...where do I go from here?
So many thoughts, so much to say,
so many things that need to be done,
a few calls that need to be made.
Chasing whatever it is that I'm chasing.
Surrendering to what I need to surrender to.
So there's still **silence**.
Silence when you think of standing
in a room amongst people,
seeing them when there is nobody there.
They are there in your hearts.
The smile is within your dreams.
The thoughts...or what you are trying

to think of what they're thinking.
Wondering about them and wondering about yourself.
There's just **silence**.
Just being able to exist knowing
that there's something that needs to be done.
Reaching out for something and not reaching.
Reaching from my heart and my soul.
Reaching within my thoughts from state to state.
Thinking about family members.
Reaching in my own home, thinking about change.
Thinking about all my friends
and family and there's **silence**.
Silence of a heartbeat that is beating within my chest.
Silence, just me thinking about all the rest.
What is the rest?
I know it's time for me to rest
because there's so many thoughts
so I guess it's time now to just dream.
So my thoughts can be a dream.
A dream of that silent dream because it's silent.
When I realize the reason why it's silent...
it's because for a hint of a second
I had a thought in between a heartbeat...
so it was silent for that moment.

Silence

K. Owens

Sunshine, the Moon, and Your Smile

12:00 a.m. I glanced over and all I saw was sunlight.

I can see the moon in your eyes

and the sunshine in your smile.

Just want you to know you're my nature,

so be patient with me

and we can grow; between you and I,

we can shine through the night.

By
K. Owens

Love is Love, Like is Like

When you love someone you love them. In order to love them you had to like them from the beginning. If you are confused about the difference it doesn't matter, because your liking someone is the beginning of loving someone. Sometimes we get confused about the differences because we think in order for us to love someone, sparks have to fly. That there has to be a sign that tells us that this is real when it's just simple. If you feel it, it's real. If you want to say it, you can't say it…that means you're beyond the like. Love is love and like is like.

We should love our parents and like the fact that they gave us love and love the fact that we can feel the love. Our sisters, our brothers, and our friends; we like that we all know each other and we have a history. Love the fact that we are not alone. There is someone who loves us the way we love them. Each and every one of us show love in different ways. One person can buy everybody gifts, and that's their way of showing. The next person can send a text message just because and that is their way. The next person probably wouldn't call or send a text, but you are thought of because all of the things that you've done in your life that they wish they could do, so you're loved just the same. Someone else can get on a flight and fly to a different state and stand in the ocean and see the most beautiful sight that eyes can see and just wish that you were there. Even though you don't know it, that's their way of saying that they love you. Love is love and like is like.

If you like to do things in your life and you love the fact that you have life, believe in something to give you reasons to want to live twice. Don't think differently of others because their love is not shown in the way that you show it — only think of the way that you show it and accept the way they are giving it. Even if it's not seen that you love them, the love should be enough because love is love.

There is no greater bond than family. There is no greater gift than true friends who became family. People outside the family have to be liked first in order to be loved and be treated as such and now they are family. Family is love from the beginning, because that's all you knew. So love is love, like is like…let's see love for what it is. Let's accept like for the word and be grateful that at least there are two. What we feel inside, no one has a greater definition of what coming together and family and love and friendship means.

In our hearts we know it because it was a gift that was given to you before you got here. So let's like each other, love each other, and accept each other for the fact that we like and we love.

By

K. Owens

Insights

Is this good enough?

I have had the great pleasure to write from my heart hoping someone felt the same. My heart beats just as well as yours, and somehow we see and hear completely different. So I take this opportunity to write words that I don't even understand just so those who don't understand can understand, and the reason why they don't understand is because my education is not on the same level. There is a meaning behind everything I write; it is because I write from pain, love, and being misunderstood, I write for the message. So I have taken this opportunity to write some big words just so the people who criticize can understand I can write on their level; I just choose not to.

Coincidences	Perception
Synchronistic	Interpretations
Encounters	Evolutionary
Destined	Evolve
Redefining	Energize
Universe	Generation
Energetic	Guidance
Perspective	Conflict
Disconnected	Mysterious

Dominating

Cultivate

Mystical

Discovering

Awareness

Transformation

Most kids in this world have to follow someone who speaks their language, and this is the language they don't understand. So I write for the kids and the adults so they don't forget the kid in them. So leave your dictionaries at home because I write from home.

Is this good enough?

By K. Owens

It is what it is

Life is unexpected. No one knows what the next minute will be. Hours, days…so it is what it is. Most of the times in life we can't change what's in the past. If it is something simple we can apologize and it can be changed because it wasn't that deep. For the most part when it is that deep, it is what it is.

We can't change the past. Facing life for what it is, understanding that there will be hate, there will be love. Crying, smiling, laughing, running, walking…hearts beating for all different reasons. Somehow we can confuse the emotions of life. When you take time just to sit down and analyze what life is, look back to the past. There are so many people who have done so many different things and worried so much about life and bills, kids, families, mothers, fathers. Where you sit or where you stand when you're reading this, those people are not here. You wonder why you worried about it anyway. If you worry about something so much to the point where it alters your life then it changes your life. If you can accept it then your life is what you make of it because it is what it is.

Smile when you hurt inside, laugh for no reason, reach out for joy in life, because you are living. Take a deep breath and feel the way your lungs in your body respond when you breathe out. Before you know it you have to breathe in again. So it is what it is. Take a deep breath, breathe for life, and breathe for you. Let's not worry about what they say, let's worry about what you think. Even though what you think can be selfish…keep yourself humble, because life is life.

Whatever purpose you have, make it the greatest purpose as long as it doesn't hurt anyone or anybody. It is what it is.

Being accused of something that you didn't do, there's no reason to argue, because if you didn't do it there should be no response but — I didn't. If there's something that you shouldn't have said but you said it anyway, own up to it because it is what it is. When you are hiding the facts it makes you look wrong, but when you speak the truth you can stand strong! Face every face as if you have nothing to hide. If there are ever any tears within your eyes they are tears of joy and tears of pain but you are being real so you will see change.

So…it is what it is.

By

K. Owens

She Makes Me Crazy

She makes me crazy from time to time.
She makes me happy when I'm sad.
I find myself trying to be mad at her just because…I
don't know why.
The only reason why I am happy —
is because I don't have a reason to cry
as long as she is in my life.
She walks like there is no tomorrow.
Her voice travels through brick walls.
Her spirit could be in another city
and I feel as if I'm right near her.
She can get in the car for no reason,
just to drive home reaching out for something.
She doesn't know what it is
but she's tired of being alone.

I have found, I have loved, and I have reminisced.

By

K. Owens

I Wish
the Phone Would Ring

If I had a wish, I would wish the phone would ring and it would
be that voice I'm missing. It would be the person I've called and
left messages for and haven't
received a return call. I was wrong.
Yes, I was wrong.
Each second is like an eternity.
I notice every button on the phone as if I've never seen it before.
I check for the dial tone just to make sure the phone works and
call the phone company to see if it's still on. I realize it has to
be, because I'm on it.
I turn it on vibrate
and put it in my pocket just so it can be close.
I am missing you.
I shouldn't have said what I said because I said it out of anger.
I shouldn't have said what I said because I love you
and I said it as if you were a stranger.
I have no excuse.
You're the closest to my heart and I took it out on you.
I am sorry in every way sorry can be said. I just wish the phone
would ring. Even if it isn't you, just the anticipation, the
thought that it could be, keeps me hoping. I get off the phone
quickly because I don't want to miss your phone call. You are
my world beyond worlds, my best friend.
I can say that I love you beyond love
and I adore you without keeping score.
But it contradicts me being angry,
saying something I shouldn't have said.
If I could rewind time, I would climb the highest mountain
and scream at the top of my lungs and through the journey of

coming down I would find some flowers
because I wouldn't have to apologize.
I can say "I've had a bad day, but this is how you make me feel"
I'm looking out my window and within seconds I think I've
counted over three thousand raindrops. It's as if I can see them
individually because I'm at one
with the tears coming from my eyes
One moment shouldn't ruin all the days and hours we spent
building our trust and our friendship.
I need to talk to you and listen more
so I can understand your side.
I can't conjure up the strength to move from this window, with
hopes of you with each light that slowly passes by. I'm still
waiting for the phone to ring…

Hello…
How are you doing? I'm glad you called.

By
K. Owens

RESPECT

To have respect you have to give respect, but first
in order to give respect you have to give respect to yourself.
If someone is wearing a janitor's outfit in the mall,
you automatically assume that person is a janitor.
But what if that person is not?
What if you walk in a place and someone has a name tag on?
Does it mean that person works there or could it mean
that they just left their job
to come in there just to buy something?
If you see someone walking down the street
with a construction hat on,
does it mean that they work construction?
All I'm saying is respect.
Respect ourselves in order for other people to respect us.

Life is not perfect no matter how we see it.
It is wrong for people to assume
that you are something that you are not
but then in the same breath you can't accuse them for being
wrong if you dress
in a way that represents you as if you are something
that you're not.
Because if you came into where I was and had a fireman's outfit,
automatically people will assume that you are a fireman.

That could be just your style, but if that's your style understand
what comes with it...if someone asks you about it,
don't be offended.
Some women are accused of being something that they're not
just by what they are wearing.
I'm not saying that it's right for them to do that,
but then in the same sense know how you present yourself,
because how you present yourself is how people treat you.
Yes it's wrong but in the same sense, you're wrong
if you don't want anyone to present you the way that you
represent yourself.

So let's have respect for ourselves.
Let's present ourselves the way
that we want people to represent us.
So if you want to be respectable, dress respectable.
If you want to be respected, be respected.
Because the way life is, people treat you
for what they see not for what they feel.
There are others who will treat you the way they feel
and they are so few and far between
but when you run into those people
that is the greatest thing.
In the same sense, life is not that way.

Let's dress the way that we want people to see us today.
Put on that outfit that represents you tomorrow
so if someone says something to you about —

Sir, can you park my car?

Make sure you are in an outfit

that parks cars and that's your job.

If someone asks you for information,

make sure you are dressed in an outfit

that says information booth.

Or if you are a fireman, police officer, street sweeper,

construction guy, delivery...

that's what it's all about.

We wear outfits because we want people to respect us for it and

that's why companies give people outfits that are different from

other people's outfits,

so they can be respected for it

when they walk in those people's stores

or when you walk in their doors.

But when we walk out of our doors,

let's be respected for who we are,

so be respected for who you are and dress for the respect.

Respect
K. Owens

Poison

Poison is in the mainstream of all the minds of the youth following those that they look up to. Alcohol, weed, methamphetamine. All of the things that changed you from reality. A gun wouldn't be a gun without bullets. Nuclear bombs wouldn't be nuclear without the bomb itself. Suicide bombers couldn't kill others if there wasn't a bomb strapped to them.

Somehow life has gotten so confused with giving you a high or something to feel good when you feel down. Something to help you get up and run faster, lift more weights, stay up a little longer when in reality it doesn't make you stronger. Man-made drugs; someone who can find the strength within them and even at their worst moment couldn't find anything, but finds something to give to you. Something to make you feel like you are somebody else. Poison to your brain. Poison, it makes the worst change. The thing that changes with you is not a good change, so you lose a big part of you.

How do we fight poison? Cigarettes serve what purpose? They kill those smoking and also kill those who stand beside you. The kids and family and friends who are breathing in the same car — they are at just as much risk as you are. For some reason your need and your greed are more important than the seed that sits and shares the same air that you do, so it's poison. Losing our brain at a rapid rate. Finding yourself doing things that you never would have done before. Waking up in places you've never been. Finding yourself interested in people that never have interested you, but you are interested in them now.

I know life is hard, but we have prayer. You have yourself and the pureness of coming into this world with the chance of being someone and being great. Somewhere along the line you got confused in order to be you; then to get over the challenges of life you have to find something to give you a little break. Not realizing that the break is the biggest mistake that you can make within your life. All those moments and seconds you are on something, searching for something so you could have a little peace, you can find what your searching for within yourself. You are only backtracking life and you're giving up your life, so don't choose the poison.

No matter how bad it gets drop to your knees and pray to the heavens, to whatever you have within your heart to believe that there can be a difference. There are so many changes in life and so much pain and death where everyone or someone is dealing with it in each second of every day. If there is one person that can come through it all clean and face it all then you can. You can crawl amongst your journey of all the things that made you fall. You can stand up in the end and be somebody. An example that it can be; so don't get lost within the poison just because of a friend who says they are a friend and it's the coolest thing to do. That is them.

Be the example. Be free and clean so they one day will want to be like you. So face the poison and say no because what you face in life are your footsteps to get to your after life. Humble yourself; face the pain. When it rains so hard where you can't see anything else, even if you don't have it you can find the strength in someone else. No matter what, you are not alone. Face the poison in your own simple way or the hardest way so you can be an example to show someone how to get home.

Face the poison.

You truly can be someone to believe in.

By K. Owens

Percentages

The percentages of life to find someone who you are compatible with — chasing a dream within a dream and trying to make things pan out to be what you see. In the same sense trying to be you and listening to someone else. I've lost; I've gained. I've lost more than I have gained, but what I have gained will give me more than I ever have lost because I've lost someone who was great to me.

She can write down all her pros and cons and I can write down mine and if we take away the color of the paper as walls that we put up and make it clear and overlap them then it will be the answer of all of our problems. Thirty percent of her strengths are my weaknesses and vice versa. Twenty percent of the things that we both doubt, we believe in. Ten percent of the reasons why we are scared is because 30 percent we know that we are right for each other. Five percent is the conversation that we have on the phone and 5 percent is the reason why we can be in the presence of someone else and still feel alone.

The only way we can see through all these percentages is to accept them all as one.

One for you, one for me, let's give this 100 percent.

Percentages

K. Owens

My Friends

If you have friends maybe this can remind you of your friends. My cousin Lee. He stood beside me, side by side. I remember days when we were eating...grape nuts and cereal with no milk, but we had the happiest times and we laughed because we had the richness of our love.

My sisters and brothers have always been close to me. It didn't matter to me whether we fought or not. I just knew our relationship has always been close because my mom wouldn't accept it to be anything different, so we grew up with that in our heart. Growing up I found many friends, and if I were to say every friend that I have, I would be telling you about friends for two days so I'm just going to mention a few...

My cousin Dahlila M. Has always been an inspiration. With a will to live beyond living because she has faced a lot and is overcame it all.

I have a friend named Kevo. His name is Kevork. If I got married today he would be my best man because he is a living example of what a true friend is.

I have a friend Deegan Wolf who stands by my side day by day. He works with me not for me. He worked for me but since our relationship became as friends, he works with me now, because friends can only work with each other and not for each other. Our relationship grows each day he is one of the biggest reasons why this book has been written. If you have a good friend I have left space towards the back of the book so you can list yours.

Melissa. She is a heavenly gift. A feather that has fallen from heaven. She has been there for me more times than ever. I remember being sick and being in a relationship with someone, and to this day I can't remember what happened, but she was the one that was there taking care of me and not my mate. So our friendship is all about faith and it's always been friends, just friends.

I think about the fathers that I've met throughout my life. The people who have touched me. I think about Van, someone's stepfather. He's the first person that made me realize life is not all about the name-brand clothes; it's about how you wear them. That was a good change for me.

My next-door neighbor, Dale, and his wife Fran. It's like a father and a mother and I try to tell them that I love them every chance that I get because they accept me for who I am and for where I am headed. They read some of the things that I write and they come over and tell me what they feel about it and it gives me the strength to want to fight harder to get it out there so the world can share.

My friend Missy has helped me throughout this book in putting it together. Some friends you just can't find the words to express so you just tell the world that they exist.

My guys on the truck that work for me and work with me side by side: Deon, Anthony, Kaston and Jesse. It's a small crew but we pack a big punch. I'm sitting here thinking about all the friends that I have, and there are so many names and so many people I can mention and it's just got me speechless.

My two sons, Matthew, Canaan — and don't take it wrong in the order that I mention my friends because this is all paper. At any given point, you can put your eyes on the paper and find a name and that will be the name. My sons are the world to me. I haven't been the best that I could be, but I'm working on it; and every day

I'm getting better at it. I know I'm not perfect, but I'm working on it. And our life goes on.

So I'm just saying every one of you have people in your life and you have friends. Let's gather them up and try to make something better than what we have. Let's remind those friends how they changed our lives because sometimes when people don't know that they made a change in you, it's hard for them to make changes in themselves and realize the worth of their friendship to you.

So I end this special thanks to my friends and the people who are dear to me and I'm saying let's all grab our wings and let's jump because it's time for us to fly free. If you miss someone, call them. If you can't call them, write them. If you have someone in your life that you love, let them know. If there's someone that you miss, let it be known.

That's why your friends are your friends, because they know that you are friends.

So let's be friends.

By
K. Owens

My Child

I love you in more ways than there are ways. I am just thankful we have days to be with each other. I wish there was a book or a magic wand to help me understand fatherhood because even I get confused sometimes about what I am supposed to and how it is supposed to be done. But I am not confused about my love for you and the passion in which I see life now because I see it differently now that you are a part of me. I can travel many miles and it seems as if my love only gets stronger and now I know how to love because once you love, your love grows and we are growing together. I close my eyes and I can see your face and the way you smile and I get caught up, lost in that daze because I don't want to open my eyes and not be able to see you. I can feel it in my heart.

Your mom she is my world even when I didn't think I can make it she gave me strength and then I knew I could, so I am not faking it, I am making it and I am taking it day by day. She has always been my rock, my passion for life even when I was the most confused, we would lean on each other. And now we have you. Now, we don't have to lean because we are a part of each other. You teach us both the greatest lesson of love because you have to show it in your expressions the way you smile, the way you laugh and also in those moments that you cry. I just want you to know we cry with you. We laugh and we smile and now we can run with no worries because through your growth you will help us tell your story. I love you.

Your Mom

Thank you for believing in me, thank you for giving me or should I say giving us our child. I feel like I was a child when we met. And I had to grow up right in front of you. I am so vulnerable at times because you know more about me than most and I love that because I adore you. I am overseas fighting for our country and our future, I took this trip for you and my child and you are missed in more ways than you know you are missed. I am so thankful because I believe in you I have no worries and my heart is at ease. I guess that comes with age and growing up with each other, it is hard for me to find the words beside I love you because I am not good with words. One thing I am good at is my faithful heart, my soft voice when I am thinking of you. I want to give you the world and at the same time I am faced with the challenges that come with this world and it isn't easy. I lay down and I close my eyes waiting for the peace and sleep to take me away so I can feel your presence in my dreams. Sometimes I toss and turn and pull the pillow close and I realize you are not there but when I open my eyes I see you were there because my pillow is wet from soft tears of thinking of you. I am counting the days to see your face and hold my child so we will be as one even though we always are, thanks for believing in me.

Your Dad

A little reminder to myself I will take everyday as it comes and be more humble about my decisions because I know the balance of life is within my footsteps and each breath that I breathe. I am not walking just for me and I am breathing for us all and no matter how heavy the world gets I will find that strength through being thankful for the blessings that have gotten me here. I will only look back to pull the strength from the days before to give me strength for the days to come. My life is about to change, my success is within reach I will grow each time I fall, I will focus when I can't see past tomorrow. I will have faith because faith is what got me here and I can only imagine how great life will be. I am thankful for the freedom of life and I am thankful to be a part of bringing life in to this world. I finally realized I don't need glasses to see the beauty in life and the strength within me. I have finally found that growth and the key is within me. To my child you can believe in me.

My Child

By

K. Owens

Lost and Found

A good reason is just because.

The real reason is searching for true love.

My reason can be satisfied with just a hug.

Sometimes when you're lost you have to be found.

I'm just searching for solid ground

and only then I shall be found.

I shall be found by a true love or a true friend,

I have faith so I spread my arms and catch the wind.

By

Kelly Owens

Me and You

There's no me without you.
I was walking today feeling the wind up against my face
while humming the Amazing Grace.
Being thankful for us and being thankful for peace.
You make me want to be a better man.
Because of you I am a better man.
You give me strength to climb any mountain,
you give me freedom to jump off the top
and spread my wings and soar.
You give me reason to never keep score,
because there is no me without you.
I can reach up and touch the sky
and at the same time give you reason not to ever cry.
So lay your head on my chest and hear my heart that
only speaks to you.
So therefore there's no me without you.
Love is a leap of faith so jump and trust you will be?

By,
K. Owens

Little Lady

Little lady you are so cute just the way you position yourself to reach something. It explains why you are such a little lady. The way you walk, the way you say what you say when you say it. Your cute attitude in those little moments when you choose to be short with your words because you feel that you've been misunderstood. Little lady you drive us all crazy.

Sister, auntie, friend...little lady I see it in your heart just in the joy you bring to us so you are our little lady. Little lady don't stress. Don't stress about the things that you can't change alone. Don't stress about the change that we have to make to make a change so we can make it. Don't stress, little lady. You drive us crazy. Little lady the way you grab your purse, tuck it under your arm, or hold it by your side we can't help but wonder what made you choose the things that you chose that you didn't want to lose tucked into that purse, because that purse is all about you. Is it your hand lotion, your face cream, your breath mints? No matter what it is, you mean something to us so you are our little lady.

Jumping out of the car just to run in to somewhere quick...calling your friends or your kids when you know they're sick...comforting us when you know that we are in pain. Little lady you've always made a change. So this goes out to all you little ladies. Little ladies getting older looking back at age, little ladies that are coming up from age. Let's turn this page to give you a reason to want to smile because we couldn't do it without you. We want to say we love you little lady. You drive us crazy.

Thank you for helping us to learn how to love because you love so deep. Your inner strength is unmatched by man because you can tolerate so much. Watching a woman carrying a child from one side of the mall to the other and showing no signs of giving up and we can't do the same because we are always looking for a change, switching our child from side to side just to make it. Little lady thanks for giving us a reason to want to dream. The desire, the passion to want to build a home. Thank you for being you and for being so cute where we don't want to be alone. Little lady, you drive us crazy. Whatever it takes for you to be you, be you. We love when we can fall in love with someone that loves us the way that you do.

Little Ladies you drive us CRRRAZY.

This is from all of the guys who dare to understand that there is a difference. Who appreciate a woman as a partner and not as an item. Who dare to understand what we don't understand and are willing to accept that it is not easy being in your shoes.
Accepting that the facts are not always the facts.
It's about feelings too.
We love you, little ladies. You drive us crazy.

By

K. Owens

I Am

When I see you, I see us.
I'm the umbrella that protects you in the rain.
I'm the one that comforts you when you feel pain.
I'm your sunglasses when there is a sun's glaze.
I'm the one that's breathing for you
when you need air.
Everything that I am is for us to share.

By
K. Owens

Help

No matter who we are, where we are headed, our financial situation, our color, race, and the country we live in — we need help. Heavenly Father, I call unto you to help. We have all grown lost within time. Trying to find ourselves and losing ourselves, trying to figure out someone else. Heavenly Father, give us a voice and a spirit and a soul to possess a word and a voice so everyone can hear and realize they should be changing life. If there's no change there will be the end of life.

Heavenly Father, help us stand and understand the weight that we stand on above the two feet that we have. Understand our purpose. Help us be willing to give in the moments when we are in need. Give us the knowledge to see through all of these confusing things that are changing us and turning us away from you. Help us.

There can't be one leader to give us a voice. Give us many so we all can have a choice and a reason to change. Some of us have been raised in such lovely homes and even then we run astray. Then there are those who have never had a home and every day are searching for one. Help us find some peace so the fighting can cease.

Lives are changing every day. So many have lost just because someone is confused in the route that it takes to get to You. We are a people and a nation in the world that You look down upon and hold in the palm of Your hand. We need Your help today…

…Please help the weak become strong.

…Please help the strong become more knowledgeable and humble
about the strength that they have
so they don't use it against the weak to feel superior.

Help them understand that we are all the same and we are all struggling for the same purpose. Each footprint that we stand in no matter what our weight makes the same print. Please help us today. Please help the ones who are reading and are listening to the silent prayer that is coming to you from someone who needs you and is willing to give whatever there is that can be given. Let the world become one and understand one another even when we don't understand.

We do understand the purpose of life, of what it takes for us to come together so that we can have life after life. Help us, Heavenly Father. Help us be able to sleep at night when our minds are so cloudy. Help carry us throughout our dreams and our nightmares and to understand that there can be a better tomorrow. Help the one man, the one woman who wants to stand above to show love and also show that they are equal.

Please help us.

Please help me.

Please help them.

Two o'clock in the morning tears running down my face. I can feel it all over my body as if I just took a bath. I'm just lost and confused. The math of adding up all the lives that are dying today and didn't understand what life is and how it should be and trying to find a way to show someone that we can be somebody so help us.

By

K. Owens

How Can We Be So Blind?

We all have been in relationships before, and for some reason we carry the baggage from before to settle the score for the ones to come. How can we be so blind? One day will be the day where we have to face what we are doing wrong so we can finally see what someone is doing right.

Being blind means that there is something that you have to find within you to see what is right for you. Falling in love and fighting love when there is so much love that has been given. Finding every excuse to run and say goodbye. How can we be so blind? Always asking for something that is so impossible for someone to give because the person that is with you could be giving it in every way. We're just so confused with how the past was that it's hard for us to see the goodness in you.

True love, real love is most likely in the person that you are seeing right now. We are just too blind to see it because we are trying to make it be the way we wanted the love to be with the person that we lost instead of accepting different love and real love from the person that we have. It will never be the same.

Love always changes. Each voice sounds different. Each laugh has a different tinkle. If we are searching for what we lost we can never find it in someone else because they are not the one who lost it; they are the ones who are giving it and we're the ones that are too blind to see it. So wake up; life is changing every day. We are losing so much every minute. We only have so much time left. The day has to come and it has to come soon when we can accept each person for who they are and not for what someone else has done. We all have made mistakes and none of us are perfect, so the only way to stay blind is by searching for someone who doesn't exist because we are not perfect. Accept someone for who they are and for the love that they are willing to give and the passion and the desire that they have in showing it. If you can accept that and accept that you are not perfect also, then love does exist. Let's not be blind.

By

K. Owens

The Key Is Within

Write from your soul, not from your pen.
Your pen is only a tool to explain
what you have within.
Let your heart guide you through the lines
as if it's your veins.
Let's write for change!
Humble your soul with glory, embrace that pen so
you can tell your story.
So therefore my life is not about a pen,
my story will be written through the changes of life.
Life is not just life, life is having life
to receive life after life.
So you can live life twice;
being born again and forgiven for our sins,
receiving the key to get in.

By,
K. Owens

The Pursuit of Happiness

The pursuit of happiness is being able to walk up to the brick wall and have hundreds of people behind you and they all see the same thing. For some reason, you see something completely different. They see a wall that has been built to keep them out. You see a wall that you need to get through to the other side so you scream and shout. You see the greater things in life...the happiness instead of the struggle. Even when you fall you start to crawl, because you'll never give up. You have a smile and you have a reason to smile because you're able to do something about it. Others can see that same wall and say there's no way we can get through. They find themselves gathering together to find the reason and a way to get past or to break it down and some just to complain. When you are standing amongst others stay humble, take a deaf ear to what seems impossible. Don't let what they say discourage you. Choose to be yourself because you know you can make it.

Finding a way when there's no way. Breaking the puzzle that can't be broke. Finding something right when it was written to be wrong. You can't climb over or break through; you realize you just put your back against it and you say it's about you. Your dreams can carry you through the brick wall to see a vision where you want to be. When you see that vision you shall be. You just have to have faith and have the spirit that can travel through walls, but only your flesh has to stand still. You have to trust and believe in one another. Believe in yourself. Even if those around you have failed, you choose to stand up even when the wall is broken. When others choose to run through, you humbled yourself and you walked through because you are grateful for each step and each brick that you step on or step over. You're telling yourself that you're better then and you will be better than whatever you had to go through to be you. Nothing can change you. From your vision it wasn't a brick wall; you just had to humble yourself to crawl. See it from a child's point of view and understand the Christ within you.

The pursuit of happiness is about chasing happiness within you when you have doubt. Chasing a smile when you have no reason to smile and laughing when you're fighting back the tears. Reaching when there's nothing to reach for. When you know there's something there. You can't grab it with your hands but you can grab it with your spirit. You can't hear it but you can feel it. A graceful walk, a soft voice, a gentle rub against your chest to feel the heartbeat. You know it's real. Believe in your heart, your soul and you can see through it. You can't see the colors or what's on the other side, but your spirit can glide through others' eyes so you can see it through them. You know within your belief Christ has given you spirit and the soul when you know your true brothers and the angels are sitting so you can see within yourself. Nothing is impossible when you're able to dream and you believe in prayers. You believe in the gratefulness within your sacrifice and humbling yourself instead of balling up your fists; you choose to relax and accept what God has given to you. You're pursuing the happiness within you because you know when you open your eyes what you see is only real if you accept it. It's fantasy once you close your eyes. You can feel your spirit and then it becomes real because you can feel it.

Accept Christ within your life. You don't have to see; you don't have to feel. You accept the gracefulness within the travels of life and you'll get through it. You are pursuing the happiness of life. What man has set before you to tell you that can't be done, you laugh as if no matter what challenge they put before you it will just be fun. Your life is beyond life because it's life with Christ. Your pursuit of happiness — you know you will live twice. Even if you fall you know there's strength within you that travels beyond the footsteps that you can actually put your foot in. You know your spirit travels beyond the stars and that's what life is all about.

Understanding that life is not about right now; it's about tomorrow. Saying goodbye to yesterday and taking the greatest things from yesterday to help you be stronger for the day to come. Being able to close your eyes and know in your heart that you will wake up to see another day. When you see life or feel the breath within your lungs, you know you've passed the test. Your pursuit of happiness has just begun.

It's all about you. What are you going to do? Are you going to listen to the others or are you going to listen to yourself? The voice that is within your head tells you something. That spirit within your heart and soul leads you somewhere else. Which would you choose? It's not a voice; it's a simple choice. Your spirit lives on even when you have passed on. Your choice is within your heart and the breath that you've taken within life can only be so many in so many days. So choose that and your spirit lives forever. Have something to believe in and you'll know what that is.

The pursuit of happiness — Thank God that I am a child of God and I've lived and experienced being a kid. To grow up to see it, to feel it, to smile and laugh about it. Face the challenges in life and shake my shoulders because I know I'll get through it. When I close my eyes and go to sleep I know I'm doing what I can to get closer to You.

Thank You, Heavenly Father, for the pursuit of happiness. I am home and I'm not alone. I'm saying it's time for others to seek what's within to come home too.

The pursuit of happiness.

I've made it and you can too.

By,
K. Owens

Wants and Needs

My view in life has always been about the things
I want and desire
and passion for the things that are dear to me.
Somehow, I'm still empty inside.
I can be driving a nice car and wanting something better.
Facing the needs is the reason for this letter.
Because finally when I receive that new car,
I find myself looking at a better one.
My desires, my passions,
and my dreams all seem as if I'm a day late.
For the first time I found out it's not about
what I want, it's about what I need.
I need you, I need love, and I need passion.
I need forgiveness and understanding
and unconditional grace,
faith, strength, and unity.
I'm thankful you finally found me.
Now I can smell your perfume
and admit it makes me humble,
because that is what I need to feel...
the presence of your being.

The space in life that we control while we are in it and
possessing ironies.
Simple terms are being more aware of your surroundings
and being in more control of your actions.
Understanding that you don't choose love,
love chooses you,
we just choose the path.
I'm just happy and thankful to be Chosen!
I know what I thank God for...unfolding my needs.

By,
K. Owens

Who Are You?

Who are you today? Are you different than who you were yesterday? I'm just trying to find out, who are you? Because in the midst of trying to find out who you are, I'm trying to find out who I am. So who are you? Are you someone who listens or are you someone who needs to talk all the time? Who are you? When you sit amongst your friends, talking about your friends, just one question to ask... who are you?

Are you better than those that you speak of or are you the same as those you speak of? And if you are the same as those that you speak of, then what you speak of should be from love and love only. So who are you?

What are you chasing? What are you accepting in your life so your life can become better? What do you believe in? Who do you believe in? Are you more superior than others? If you are, then why are you talked about? No one has ever walked this earth and been so precious to the point where the tongue has never lashed them by the things and the choices that they've made. We are not perfect; you are not perfect. Someone has made a decision that you might not agree on. It's not for us to accept it or to judge it. What we can do is what we can do for ourselves and the ones who are true friends within our lives made a decision to change their lives. So I'm asking you, who are you?

If you walked in the room and there were one hundred people that you've never seen and everyone in there was a different nationality and believed something different than what you believed, would you feel comfortable within your skin? If you do, why and if you don't, how come? Everyone sees something different within others. We all believe different things when we all believe the same things. Sometimes we get lost in the midst of the dark, trying to find our light. Sometimes the light is not what we should be searching for. We should be searching for ourselves. Sometimes the greatest find that can ever be found is within the darkness of finding yourself, so you can shine through the night to show others a way. So who are you? There always can be a change in life. It can start right now. No matter who you are or how you are or what you believe in... your life can change within a split second. From the moment this page releases from your fingertips you can only have so long to live. Then again, you can have long to live.

So who are you to be you so you can be you when it's time for you to find you? So let's find it. And the best way to find you is not compare yourself to anyone else, because every time you judge someone and say that they shouldn't have, they couldn't have, and you don't understand why they did...you lose a part of you. That energy that you have that is worried about them and the choices that they made is strength that you've taken from yourself to climb that hill to find yourself. So by being you, it's the strongest rope that can ever be laid down on the side of a mountain for someone who is lost to climb up. So be you.

Let's trust and believe that every decision that you make is not going to be right. Every thought that you have in your head is not the greatest, but it can be the latest that brings you to the point where you can find something that is right for you. Pick up a Bible; pick up something that is something to you so you can find something to help find out. There's nothing wrong with being lost. The only time something can be wrong with being lost is not having the energy to find yourself when you are lost because you're so worried about someone else and the decision that they've made. So I'm asking you, who are you? When it comes time for you to find who you are, let's not let it be the last minutes of your life of knowing who you were. Who are you?

Life is about minutes and seconds and it's all about time. So find it while you have time. Let's not face it confused when we have no time.

I'm asking you...Who Are You?

By
K. Owens

Inside Out

Learning how to love. It's time...it's time for us all to come together. Start paying more attention to the things that are around us. It seems as if we are missing the big picture

Don't judge a book by its cover, because no matter what the cover says, you can be misled if you formed your own opinion before the book is read.

Our mind takes us on journeys where most the time we don't want to go but we end up going there anyway, because we let our eyes deceive us. The best thing is to see it with your eyes and process it with your heart and let your soul and your spirit guide you through it. Because the most important things are from within. Your heart has so much love to give...at least it should have so much love to give, and if it doesn't, you need to make a change!

Let's look at things differently. Looking at the oranges; it's as if you want to say a prayer before they were planted. Just let your crop know that there is a hard journey ahead. The outside skin of an apple is not the best, but you bite into it and you taste something completely different than what you see. That orange has weathered the storm. If you look real close you'll see the dents, you'll see the scars, and if you peel it you'll get something so sweet, but you have got to pick it at the right time.

Anything you find in life that's right in front of us...it's the inside that matters. So why do we choose to judge people by what we see from the outside? Let's not! Grab a bottle of lotion. It's not about the outside of the lotion; it's what is inside. It could be the greatest name on the outside of that bottle, but if the inside doesn't represent the outside, you're disappointed. Perfume, a cologne bottle has the best design, but if it doesn't smell right it's not for you. But if you buy it just for the shape, you smell completely different than what you want to smell. Would you do that? Is it worth it to buy something just because of the beauty of the bottle and not care what's on the inside? Because if you buy it just because of the beauty of the bottle, then keep it for whatever it is. Don't touch the inside. Use it just so the eyes can see. If you want what's on the inside, it doesn't matter what the bottle looks like.

So let's take a walk through the grocery store. Everything is packaged in some kind of wrapper one way or the other. Cereal is in a box, laundry detergent is in a container, toothpaste is in a tube, and you choose how you're supposed to view things. You view it from within. Because the best of the best comes from the inside. The outside weathers the storm to reel you in.

Let's be a friend to a friend. It doesn't matter what clothes they have on their body. All that matters is their heart and the drive that they have in life, and just because they don't have it today doesn't mean that they're not your friends tomorrow. Let's help them. Let's be there. Even at times when we're weak we can be strong. As long as you have knowledge of something, you have information to change somebody.

If you speak it, your voice comes from the inside and it parts your lips and it's heard by ears or the vibration that is accepted by somebody else in order for what you said to be processed from the inside. So don't view things from the outside. Let's work on it together. We can do it. Shoes don't mean anything unless you put your feet on the inside. A shirt, clothes don't mean anything unless your body's on the inside of them. So it's the inside that matters most about the outside. You need to take care of the outside so the inside can grow. Take care of those clothes so you can protect your skin in the sun. Keep those shoes clean so they can protect you when you're walking up and down the street. So your inside is supposed to be strong enough to make the outside stronger. By being strong you're getting nicks, dents, scratches, scrapes. You don't look the same as you when you came off the assembly line, but your heart is so defined...pumping that blood through your veins. You see people from the inside and you struggle to change.

So close your eyes and see it from within.

Inside Out

K. Owens

Our Moms Raised Us Better Than This

Press rewind back to the days of our relationship. We had the best of times. I remember us watching karate movies and hanging out downtown. We dressed alike; we both had those Michael Jackson jackets and spent our last dimes just to get them. We were so alike because our parents instilled the will to fight and work together. I remember us cooking French toast. We must've gone through two loaves of bread. There wasn't a basketball or football that we didn't play with together. You were better at basketball than I was, so you taught me how to play. Do you remember the football team that we played on? We were the best. There wasn't a time I fell and you didn't catch me or help me get up and me the same for you. It seemed as if life didn't exist if we weren't together. We would sit and listen to your mom's records: O'Brien, Rick James, Betty White. I remember your first car and your stereo; you could not be beat. We would listen to Dizzy Phillips. I remember your first job.

What's so weird is I know nothing about you now. If your mom and mine were still in their thirties we both know we would have our tails whipped for the distance we have between us. Tough Love. They both sacrificed to give us life. I just want you not to forget the good old days. It never cost us anything to be who we are to each other. To this day I see you as a brother and nothing less. It hurts every time I see your mom's eyes. It brings tears to mine. We owe it to our kids for them to know each other. There can't be that much hate in the world for us to take that from them. Matthew's number is 000-0000 and Canaan's number is 000-0000. No excuses! They will love your kids like brothers and sisters. All I need to know is when and where and they will be there. If not through me, through them.

These are the same words and things that we have been taught all our lives. I can only admire your fatherhood from afar because I never see your face. You will always be a part of me in every way. Life without life I can't understand because I have thirty-something years watching you grow from a boy to a man. I want life with life, so let's live our lives. Your brother James has been a great friend through this all. His voice is the only way for me to know how life is for you and your family. I thank him for that. At this point you only owe the attorney and then it's over.

I pray for you and your family every day that I pray for mine. I want you all to have the greatest success. Just as much as you love your family, that's how much I love you and yours. All I ask is let's face the man that we see in the mirror and I know it would help us see a little clearer. Focus on who we are and how much our childhood means to us and see what our mothers were willing to die for just so we can live. Family is family, love is love, and true friends will never see an end when love comes from within. I cry about all that I missed because all I have is past time to reminisce. Sometimes I look in the mirror and my eyes are blurry and I ask God how did it come to this? It seems while I'm writing this I can see us laughing and picking on others, just making fun. I miss us just being one. If you choose to or choose not, just remember Our Moms Raised Us Better Than This.

Kelly Owens

Facing the World

I woke up this morning
and I felt as if I could conquer the world.
Giving the world the best of me
for the things I believe in.
I want to run and dance with joy in my heart
because I know passion
and life will live forever.
Thanks for making me smile.

K. Owens

Excuses, Facts, and Reality

Excuses are searching for reasons why.

Facts are explaining why.

The reality is…

It doesn't matter what your excuses are, or

your facts...it didn't get done.

So therefore there are no excuses.

K. Owens

Consistent

Are you consistent in being consistent? Being someone who can be counted on; or are you consistent in not being consistent? If that's the case you are consistent in something. But it is not the consistency to be proud of. The hardest thing to read is when the truth lies hidden in the words. And while you are reading you can feel proud or you can feel guilt and if you are proud no word has to be changed. But if there is guilt you are changing the sentence to benefit you.

Consistency

By K. Owens

Time

It's time for us all to come together. It's time to weather the storm. It's time to be embraced by the ones that you love within their arms. It's time. The world is getting crazy and everything is changing. What used to be good is not good anymore. Being safe is all about being selfish in some ways, which is sad. It's time to go home. It's time to wake up. It's time for us to start to crawl. It's time to stand and try to walk. It's time to learn what speech is and put words together to try and talk. Mama, daddy, sister, brother. It's time to love one another. It's time. You find yourself working, looking at the clock waiting for it. It's time to go home. Waking up in the morning, hitting the snooze button because it's almost time to get up and go to work. To get up to do something. It's time to put on those clothes, to wash your face and brush your teeth. It's time to make those phone calls. It's time for all of us.

So what does time mean to us? How much time do we all have? Individually each one of us has a certain time. How much time is that? Someone is driving down the street talking on a cell phone, listening to someone on the other line saying something to them. Their response is — I'll get to it later because I have all the time in the world. It seems as if all the time in the world was just a second because time didn't exist after that phone call. That is sad. None of us know how much time we have. You hear it on TV every day. Someone just running to the store and now they'll never face another day. People falling asleep and not waking up. It's time. I think it's about time for us to find what's best for us at the time that we think of time. We get our hearts right. We search for our glory. We live every second and minute with footsteps through our life to tell our story. It's time to get ready. So when it's your time you are ready.

We all take our seconds and minutes for granted because we are strong. Somehow we think we have the strength to live on forever. Deep in the back of our minds we know it won't last but we never think it will happen to us, and then one day it does and then we think back wishing that we had more time. So time is for us to find the time and make the time to get your heart right, your soul on board, and your spirit to the point where everyone throughout the valley can hear it and feel it. Be real about what you believe in. Strive to achieve what's great in your life. Let your name be a legacy that is for change, and that change will change you and change others. It's time.

Looking up at the clock and it seems as if it's forever for five minutes to pass and then in the same sense when I'm running late, five minutes is the quickest time to come. Sometimes I wonder why that is. So I have to start taking care of my seconds so my minutes are right, and when my minutes are right I have to fight for my hours, and when I receive my hours it's time to get on board so I can see my days. When I'm breathing and experiencing the day before me ...it's time to be humble praying for another day. Another week and a month. When that month comes I should be saved. I should be saved before I was saved, but it took me time to find the time to make the time so I can have the time to be saved when I should've been saved from the beginning. I thought I lost time throughout the journey. I wouldn't have had time to be saved.

It's a sad thing everybody. We've gotta make the time and the time is now. While your ears are hearing this being read or your eyes are processing the words upon this page, just as quick as it goes through your eyes into your brain to process what has been said, it's time for you to be saved because you're away now. Tomorrow you could be dead. So it's time. Let's find it. There are so many great things in this world that can happen. There's so many tragic things that can and in the midst of both we have to find something within us. At the same time it's all about what time we have left and the sad thing about it is we never know. So by not knowing right now, it's your time. It's time to have time to find Christ in your life and be thankful for you're next second leading up to your next minute.

Heavenly Father, we come to you not knowing the next minute, hours, or days that are laid out for us. We come to you humble to be accepted so we'll be grateful for those days to come. So when the time comes for us to go home we've given the time and embraced the moments. Humble with joy and being able to forgive and try to understand the things we don't understand. We're thankful for what we do have. Grateful for the times to come. We'll give you glory for a chance for our story to be told. For the moments that we have been able to walk through someone's door and our presence to be felt. Our smiles to be remembered, our laughter to be heard through the walls and through the trees. The essence of our being to be remembered throughout people who pass by and don't know us at all but feel the spirit within. We're thankful for those minutes. Give us the strength and the knowledge to come together now.

Give us the strength to bow down and understand that it is now for us to get our lives right; not tomorrow because we are not promised tomorrow. The only promises that we can keep are the promises that have passed. So thank you for the moments for us to fulfill the promises that we have said and help us be able to see one another no differently than we see ourselves. We have to walk and feel the spirit for what is to come and to be ready when our time is done.

In Lord, Jesus Christ's name we pray, Amen.

By
K. Owens

Something We Should All Say to Our Kids

Life is not perfect.
We all have done wrong.
We have to deal with challenges of life, but we love you,
and that's the reason why we are all here today,
because of the love that we have for one another.
If you think you got away with
what you are thinking about doing
or what you've already done —
Just because we didn't see it
doesn't mean you got away with it.
And if you can get away with what you're thinking about
or what you've already done without Christ seeing it,
then I support you.
But until then, **tough love**.
You're grounded; go to your room.

K. Owens

What Do You Think?

Arguing for no reason. It's either what I said or the way I said it or how you said it or the tone that's in your voice. Two people who love each other and miss each other to the point where their day can't go on. We find ourselves arguing. There's no reason for us to argue in the first place. Is it because I didn't call you this morning or because you didn't call me this evening? One way or another we know we love each other so it doesn't matter. Sometimes in life you get caught up in life, with work and trying to survive. You might miss a phone call or two but you aren't going to lose just because of that.

Your attitude is something that I don't understand. My attitude I know you don't understand, but the love that we have for each other is understood instantly. We miss each other and find ourselves getting upset because the other person didn't call when at that same moment we should pick up the phone and make that call. We realize that it takes two. It's not about who called first; it's about the fact that you called and there was an answer or an answering machine. One way or another that's what life is all about. So I don't want to argue anymore. I want to find a solution to the reason why we get upset and be complete for the reason of getting through it. I'm sorry for the days that I walked away when I knew I missed you every step of the way. Wondering what you were doing, what you were thinking, and hoping that you were wondering the same.

Every time my phone rings I'm hoping that it's you. I changed your ring that was a special ring to the same ring of others just so I have to actually look at the phone to see who's calling because when it rings and it's not your ring I get sad. If your ring is the same as others just the percentage that it could be you is well worth the change in changing that ring. So I miss you and I want to say that I'm sorry. I want to work on this and I hope you want to work on it also.

Let's make a change and let's not be upset because this is life.

So what do you think?

By

K. Owens

How Can I?

How can I walk away and never look back?
How can I look away when it's so hard?
How can I breathe
when I'm not used to breathing alone?
How can I face time when every minute I'm fighting
not to pick up the phone?
So you tell me, how can I?
How can I look away
when you are a big part of who I am today?
How can I sit at home and be in the presence of
someone and still feel alone?
How can I go to work with a smile on my face
when there's so much pain?
Why do I walk outside in the rain and not need an
umbrella because I want the rain to fall on my face?
Why do I get in the car and not put on my seat belt?
Why do I fall asleep in the tub thinking about lost love?
How can I move on when I hear so many songs that
remind me of the best?

Why can't I put my heart to rest?

By

K. Owens

It Wasn't Me

When I see you, I see us.

When I see you, I see pain.

I see you so happy and so sad at the same time

and it's hard to understand how those two can co-exist.

You tell me how you used to be.

You tell me how you were hurt.

You tell me about all the pain, but in some ways,

I've been through somewhat of the same.

I just want you to know, it wasn't me.

You had so much joy in your heart.

You laugh as if there is no tomorrow

but the sadness of your face can take so much away.

I'm confused.

I don't know whether to walk up and give you a hug

or turn and walk away

because you are pushing for your space.

I just want you to know it wasn't me.

All the time that we spend laughing, talking...

it's meant for something.

Just because you feel alone, doesn't mean

that you are alone.

In order for love to exist, someone has to open the door so

love can be invited in.

But at this point regardless of what we go through,

I'm glad that I am your friend.

I just want you to know, it wasn't me.

It wasn't me that put you through all the drama.

It wasn't me that gave you all that pain.

It wasn't me that walked out and didn't look back.

I just want you to know, it wasn't me.

There's a future ahead.

You have to open your eyes in order to see it.

You have to open your heart in order to feel it.

Embrace that feeling from within and you can feel the wind

upon your face.

There always can be a change...

you just have to rearrange the pain

because this relationship is not the same.

You have to say goodbye to old habits

and hello to new ones.

If you used to be a certain way and you've changed

because you were hurt,

then I am paying for something that someone else has done.

All I'm telling you is, **it wasn't me.**

There have been a lot of days

where you just want to be alone.

Just don't forget when you're alone, I'm alone.

You say I can never understand and you're probably right.

In most situations I'm not supposed to understand.

I'm supposed to stand by you, beside you,

comfort you through the moments.

I know everything that I go through, you don't understand.

It's a waste of breath.

For it to be bitter, first trying to understand one another

when one is in pain.

When love is involved you have to realize...

you are not supposed to understand.

That's what being there for each other is all about.

It's being there when you don't understand

and being there when you do.

I'm just saying, it wasn't me.

It's amazing how the person

before me is messing it up for me

when this relationship and the time

that we have right now is for us.

Hmm...it seems as if it was

that bad there should be room to move on.

A relationship is all about timing

and it's not time when the moon

and the stars are all lined up together.

The time is when you make the time at times,

when you feel that you don't have the time.

That's what's real.

It's better to work it out than to shout it out.

I just want you to know, it wasn't me.

By

K. Owens

Life Can Be So Crazy

Life can be crazy if you're seeing it from someone else's accomplishments. Their fortune and fame or their downfalls. Either way it's not your fortune and it's not your fall. It is your fall if you choose the fortune and you do fall because you were searching for someone else's dream.

Life can be crazy. Life is crazy when you are thinking of life and all the crazy things that are going through life. The people down the block, the people in the stores, the commercials on the TV, or what you hear on the radio. So many things to confuse you of who you are. You are who you are when there is no music, no TV, and it's just you and you can be you. Standing in the mirror looking at yourself. What are you going to do to change you so you are someone that someone else will listen to and want to be like? If that's the case what example and what would you like to be said about you when you are searching for love, success, food on your table, love from your family... giving, taking, confused, committed?

There are so many things in life that we're faced with. Don't think you're less than a woman or a man just because you're confused. We all have to deal with feeling so healthy one day and so bad the next. It's about what we breathe, what we eat, what we want to achieve, and all our downfalls and our accomplishments. In the same sense, we have to find who we are. That can be so hard and it can be so easy.

When you're running a race with someone else, you run faster when they run faster. When they run slower you find yourself running a little slower even though you still want to beat them. When you're running against yourself, no matter how fast you run, you're running pace by pace. No matter how slow you run, you're running slow right next to yourself. No matter how you wipe your eyes or lotion your feet, it's a mimic of yourself so there's nothing to be defeated. The greatest challenge is to face yourself to see who you are so you can be a better person.

Chasing someone else's dream is not a dream. Chasing your own can be a reality and it can be a strength that someone else can see from behind and say I want to be like you. Find yourself even if you have to lose yourself because we all have to be lost in order to be found. The greatest find is when you find yourself, because it's more than platinum and gold. It's the greatest self-accomplishment that you can ever have. It's the greatest story to be told. Choose the height that you want to jump. Choose how low you want to go, and if you want to crawl, let it be your choice. If you fall, say I can get up on my own. Prepare yourself before you fall. If you're standing, be grateful that you are. If you see others, believe in them just as well as you believe in yourself. In order for them to believe in you, they have to feel the belief within you, so believe in them also. Give them the path to see that there is trueness within you.

Sometimes, being lost, you can also lead someone to be found as long as your heart and spirit are grounded by someone that is true and that is you. Reach out, speak out, and hum if you don't know the words. Find that melody that represents the story that needs to be told about you and just hum it. Even if no one else knows it they can feel it. Even if you don't know the words because the words have never been spoken, give them the reason to want to go to heaven to hear it. Trust within your spirit. Believe in you. Believe in others. Believe in yourself so you have reason to believe in someone else and they have a reason to believe in you. The goodness in life lies within everyone, so even when you see someone doing something wrong, you don't look down or up. Just be an example, because sometimes being an example helps them to realize what life is supposed to be. Believe in yourself so others can believe in you. Believe in Christ through your spirit so even if you don't know it you can feel it and they also can. There is a path that helps everyone find a way to find themselves so we all can be somebody in the short time we have.

I am somebody and you are too.

By

K. Owens

I Woke Up

I woke up this morning and I had a bad dream last night
but it's okay because I'm awake.
So it doesn't matter what that dream was.
Because a dream that's within a dream is a dream that I am
because I am awake and I'm happy.
I have a chance to do it again or to make different choices, to
hear different voices.
I can get up and go to work.
I can see the sun shine.
I have a chance to see the moon glow.
I am awake.
I am thankful.
Thank you, Heavenly Father. Thank you, Jesus, for the moment,
for the time that it took for me to be awake again.
So I'm going to call somebody.
I'm going to call my mom or maybe my sister or my brother
but I'm going to call somebody.
Because if you can hear this, if you can read this,
you should be happy too because you are here.
Just while your eyes are following the words on this paper,
you can see this, you can feel it.
Can you feel that paper in your hand?
Can you feel it?
Can you feel those clothes on your back?
That's how I feel; I hope you can feel the same
because I'm happy.
No matter how bad things were or have been,

I'm happy that I am here.
Because I have a chance to do it all over again.
Can you see it?
Obviously you can because you're reading this
or you are hearing this.
One way or another, you are here.
So let's be thankful.
I want to either run outside or I'm going to run in the kitchen
and cook me some eggs
or make me a bowl of cereal but I'm awake to have a choice.
To eat that or cut a slice of cake.
I'm here and I'm happy about that.
I can live with that and I hope you can too
because you are you and you are here so let's do it together.
Let's do it together.

One more day is what we have, and let's pray for more to come.
For while we have this day let's be happy about it.
Our friends, our family, no matter what it is...ups, downs,
smiles, frowns...
it doesn't matter. We are awake.
So no matter what it is. let's be happy to deal with it
because we are here TO deal with it and we have a chance to
sleep again.
Let's pray for the time that we'll be awake again.
So we are starting all over again.

By
K. Owens

My Best Friend

My best friend is someone that believes in me in the same manner that I believe in them. My best friend is someone when I think of them, I think of me also because we are no different but we are different, and our difference is the reason why we are best friends because we see no difference within each other. We accept each other for our differences so truly that she is, he is, my best friend.

My best friend can be someone who doesn't see what I see and how I see it. My best friend is someone that I believe in even in moments when I don't believe in myself. My best friend.

My best friend is someone that I'm confused about at times from the decisions that they make, and I stand behind them anyway; but I'm honest with them about my opinion, whether it's right or wrong. So truly I love my best friend.

My best friend is someone that I can talk with about anything and everything in my life and not be judged, just understood. Even if I'm not understood, they understand. That's why I love my best friend.

I would love to have a best friend like that at all times. I'm grateful for the ones that I do have that are my best friends. So if you have a best friend, believe in them. A best friend is someone that you believe in and it's not physical. It's more spiritual. It's something that you can believe in just for the thought and the feeling that you have of knowing that they are there, and when you feel the wind upon your face, you know that you're not alone. When that phone rings and you hear their voice, no matter what it said, you know you're on the way.

Having a best friend is something to cherish. Within your lifetime you only have so many, and if you're sitting back critiquing everything that someone does around you as if you would've made better decisions, then it's hard for you to have a best friend. In that same situation you aren't your best friend because no one is better than the other even if your decision is better. Because your decision is better only in your eyes. My best friend is my best friend because my friend is my friend and through my life and the way that I live my life, our friendship will never come to an end.

K. Owens

Your Own Words

You search to find something and even when you find it,

you find yourself doubting that you were even searching.

So therefore you're not searching and in your own way you're hoping.

But even when there's hope, there's doubt.

You say you want so many different things from someone.

You have this great resume and theirs is the same, but when it's

presented to you instead of giving an interview you go back to the old

you because you wished they

would have noticed you in the beginning.

Your own words.

Many times we create a future because of our past.

While those doors have shut, the person

that you want is standing right there.

When you see them walking away, as if they've had enough, you open

up those doors and ask them to come back.

When there's no response, you hear your own words coming from

them as if you said it.

You've created a distance, but you want to hold someone close.

You say what you need but you don't act on what you want.

Your mind can only be read if you put it down on paper,

but as long as it stays in your mind there's nothing to find.

You find yourself saying, "he didn't do this" or "she didn't do that".

In your own words you didn't either.

Only your true friends know you're in love and

the one you love only knows of your past and your pain.

And when the tables are turned, it is easy to point the finger and say

"this is what you didn't do and this is how you made me feel" when

you should be saying it to yourself, because it is reality,

because both situation are real.

Because you both were right and you both were wrong.

If you can finally put down the score card and talk about the future,

you might just realize that your past can't be so bad if it led you to

cross each other's path.

You can focus on the present without any influence

of the pain you inflicted on

yourself or that you inflicted on each other.

There can be a birth of a great future ahead.

But until then, you both will remain friends and one day what you

have will come to an end.

How bad do you want what you're about to lose?

Step up to the plate and give a real interview from the real you.

In your own words.

By
K. Owens

When You Have Kids

Kids can be kids. Babies are babies. In the midst of growth you find yourself wondering if you're crazy. When they're fed, changed, and set on your shoulder or your knee to burp, you're the one that has to be alert for every movement. Checking to see if they have a fever or an ear infection and even if they have been changed, you have to check and see if they have to be changed again. Throughout all that, your work is not done. Whether you have a daughter or a son, this is the beginning of life. Teaching how to crawl, how to speak, and before that how to eat. Dealing with life that has to do with you so you can be stronger so you can be you. Then your child can be someone. Days and months mimic each other, and before you know it your child is speaking to you in the same words as your sisters and brothers.

Being a mother or a father. It's not an easy route to take. It's a blessed route because it's fate. It's a blessing of someone coming into this world, and it doesn't matter whether they're a girl or a boy. All of a sudden there's a ring and it's a bell. It's time for school. Now they have to follow someone else's rules, which are somewhat similar to the ones they have at home.

Being a parent. It isn't easy to do it on your own. It's not easy when your kids are grown. You buy shoes today and they don't fit next week. Days and months pass by. Their homework is past the education that we had. We struggle to maintain. We figure it out in our own way. Today is the day. We face that our kids are getting older and we have to take a step back to see all the work that we've done and be proud for our daughter or our son.

Heavenly Father, for all the prayers that we've prayed throughout the years. For all the times that we shed that river of tears. Please give our child the strength to be able to face reality and maintain their sanity. To understand no matter how confused they get they have a loving home. For them not to ever forget all the moments that we've been through to get through so they can be themselves.

That's what we're all about. Life is about our kids. Setting an example and paving a way so they can have a more productive life and be more prepared for the life to come.

Heavenly Father, we thank Thee for the days before and the days throughout and the present day that we live in. We pray that our kids grow throughout the tough love and as always the real love. The challenges for our love to bring us closer so the challenges that we have within the world don't pull us apart.

We thank Thee.

By,
K. Owens

I Feel Like

I feel like our relationship is more like a jump rope. I'm always trying to jump in. I'm always standing on the outside, no matter what I say. The rope still begins and it never ends. My conversation and what I have to say for some reason is always important for something that you have to say.

Where does is start? Where what I have to say begins? Because as soon as it begins, it comes to an end. I can see red and you can find something in your life that is about red. Or I can see blue and it's about you. I can see yellow and it's not your best fellow. I can see brown and it's about something that you found. I'm just a little lost, not knowing when to jump in because I want my voice to be heard. I don't want to be one part of a conversation. I want to be able to jump in and be a part of a conversation. When I say yellow I want to talk about the fellow that I ran into today. When I say brown I want to talk about what I found. When I say blue, maybe I just might want to talk about you. Sometimes all it takes is just to listen.

I feel as if sometimes I'm alone. Nothing matters when it's about me and my home or my family. Everything that goes through my family, whether it's a kid riding a bike or someone flying a kite or some lady who cooked a cake, it's all switched around to something that is on your plate. You have someone who flew a kite and flew it higher than mine. Or you have a kid on your block that rides a bike and jumps across the street. I'm just saying, I want to be a part of the conversation. I don't want to be alone, sitting in your home, because I can be alone sitting in my own.

So all I say is, sometimes it's time to listen, because sometimes when you listen you learn so much. The things that are about your life are about your life, but the things about my life and other people's lives can actually change your life and give you different views and different things to choose. So all I'm saying to you is...

Listen without a quick response. Listen to understand and understand who I am and where I'm coming from and what I'm trying to say and the picture that I'm trying to paint to you today. Then we can talk about your day because your day has always been important to me because I hear it everyday and all day. I know how this happened, I know how that happened. I know all about the past. I know all about the glass that you bought or the things that you thought, but you know nothing about me. The only things that you know about me are the things that I start to say or the things that I begin but you never hear the end.

So all I'm saying is listen, just listen, because what I have to say is important to me. I have so much that I want to show and tell but I can't say it. I just can't say it because I can't get a word in. Like I said it's like jump rope; I can't jump in. So let me be a part of your conversation by you listening.

Just listen and then you will learn.

Then I will listen to you like I always do.

By,
Kelly Owens

I'll Never Give Up

I'll never give up anything when it comes to us. The thoughts, the memories, and the days to come. I'll never give up. When I'm asleep and dreaming, so many things pass through my head, when I'm covered or just tucked in bed. No matter what my dreams are or where they take me, I will never give up. When I get up I'm thinking of you. I just want you to know I'll never give up.

Going places, seeing so many different faces. Different people, different religions. Kids, family, different cars. All the name brands that people have chosen for the name brand or just for the looks. There are so many things in this world that can take you from what true love is because everybody is going so fast. I just want you to know that I've slowed life down to the point where everything is in slow motion because I'm focused on you. No matter what passes me by, my eyes are focused on you. If I can't see you, my heart beats for us. When I can feel the wind against my face or blowing across my arms or my body, I know there is somebody that I am in love with. I want you to know — I'll never give up. Tripping, falling because I've lost my way sometimes from day to day. Even the times that I've lost have a vision where I should be headed to be found so I'm never giving up.

Sitting at the counter, eating licorice. The TV is on, people are whispering and talking in the other room. Somebody is playing on the computer, and I can hear the water in the bathroom because somebody is taking a shower. Even though I'm surrounded by so much I don't forget your touch. Your smile, your perfume, the essence of your being and your spirit that you glide through this world on. I just want you to know I will never give up.

I can't give up because I know what is true. I can't give up because I know I'm in love with you. I can't give up because God has given me a purpose to change life. Just the thought from time to time I'm just wondering if you'll ever become my wife so I can't give up. I can take you as a friend, I can take you as a mate — either way I can relate because if that's the way it is it'll just be fate. I believe the way a heart beats and the way you walk and the way the wind blows. No one knows the next minute or hour he has to hold but I do know I can have it unfold the future. I believe in what's great, and I believe in you. I believe in Christ. I believe in searching for things within your heart to give you that tingle. Searching with your eyes closed and reaching out with your fingertips. If you can't touch it there's no rush because you do believe that you will achieve. I will never give up.

At the end of the day, lights are being cut off; kids are prepared for bed, another day to face. Another night begins, and closing my eyes I'm thinking about all my true friends. The ones who are close and the ones that are just friends. Either way I'm thinking of you or I'm thinking of them. Soft pillow, dimming the lights, sleep timer on the TV just so I don't have to remind myself to get up to turn it off.

I'm never giving up, because I change every day. I'm never giving up because I'm lying down to sleep and I'm praying for another day. I can close my eyes and take my last breath and I'll be okay with that. If I wake up and have another breath then I'm in love with that so I'm in love with you. I'm saying good morning, sweetheart.

I'll never give up.

By,
K. Owens

I Believe in My Blessings

Today I smiled about yesterday

because yesterday was all about us.

Tomorrow is about our future.

My sunshine is just as bright at night as it is during the day,

because you bless me this day.

So I say thank you for yesterday, thank you for today,

and I will love you for forever and a day.

I loved yesterday and today.

They will always be done the right way.

I'm not afraid to think about yesterday or last week.

I'm humble with joy because I have you in my life.

Monday through Sunday, it seems as if it's one day.

I found the secret that there is no yesterday

without tomorrow to follow.

There is no sunset without the moon to follow.

All the days will stay the same; it's up to us to make the change.

I am blessed and I'm looking forward to my tomorrow.

By
Kelly Owens

Why Do I?

Why do I fight for change?
Why do I stand and face the pain?
Why did I bow my head in shame?
How come I feel as if the world can be changed and it has to be
from someone who's not afraid of walking in the rain?
Why do I think about the things in my life that I miss?
Why do I sit at home and reminisce
of all the family and friends that I miss?
Why do I not pick up the phone and just make that call?
Why do I want to fight for change?
The change has to start with me.
Because in order for me to stop asking myself why,
I have to face the love and embrace the love and look within
therefore there will be a change.
I will finally pick up that umbrella to protect me in the rain
and hold my head high so I can see a change.
Change is the ingredient to conquer the pain.
So now I don't have to ask why...
because I know the answer lies within me.

By
K. Owens

College

Another day's stress and I'm giving it my best.

Chasing my education with intelligence to succeed.

Responsibility of having a job and having to study in the same breath.

I don't know whether to smile, cry, or jump for joy because I'm facing it head on.

I believe, you believe, we believe so we shall succeed.

Graduation... the job I desire with the relationship and peace from above.

Now that's how I got through college.

By
Kelly Owens

Given

I have reason to smile when I think of you.

I laugh about the times when we were one on one.

I have joy when I know I'm going to see you soon.

I get the chills 'cause your heart is something I

would like to steal.

I don't like being in that position 'cause the heart is

something that should be given.

By

K. Owens

How Do We?

How do we get through this?

We can sit and have so much fun.

We can laugh as though it's our last one.

We can hang out all day like best friends.

You can tell me all the things

that you like about me and I can say the same to you.

Our love is like the wings of a butterfly.

No wing is ever the same.

And every time it takes flight, it's flying for change.

Two different colors that represent our personalities, and each

time the wing flaps down it takes us farther from the ground.

We need each other because we can't fly with one wing.

By

K. Owens

Twisted Story Lost Within the Wind

Two men fighting over the same woman. One loves for the lust of love, the other loves because there isn't anything else but love. One knows there is another; the other loves her like he loves his own mother. The woman in the middle has nothing to lose; because what she doesn't get at home she has another to choose. She's a girlfriend to one and a wife to the other.

Anger from being betrayed; lust because of the rush of cheating and no trust. Two hearts beating for the same heart that is cheating. One man knows the truth, and he is no better than the woman who tells the lies and searches for her alibis. In the end, someone gets hurt or someone dies, either way someone cries. Two men face to face, as the truth unfolds. Girlfriend and wife — someone's life is in the balance of change.

One has a brick, the other has a knife, both facing each other; it's not a fair fight. So here comes the gun; the balance of life could be faced with the last sunset, because a life can be taken and the freedom of one will be gone. The gun represents cheating; the bullet represents the two men, melted down with the heat of anger and being betrayed to form a bullet. Sucked in by passion and love into a shell, the gunpowder represents the woman.

Then there is a gunshot. The shell is the husband that is the most innocent, now guilty. The bullet is a part of the man lying down. The gunpowder is the woman lost within the wind, searching for the comfort of a new friend. The powder can cry and tell how the story began and say I don't know what happened he was just my friend. So it was said.

The man lying down has no story to tell. The shell that is in jail is confused because he doesn't know where his marriage fell. A sad, sad story that shouldn't have had to be told so be true and a different story will unfold.

Twisted story lost within the wind.

By,
K. Owens

Commitment

Commitment can be seen in so many different ways. Commitment to your sisters, your brothers, your friends, families, your husband or your wife, girlfriend and boyfriend. Commitment is what you make of it. Everyone has their different opinion of what a commitment is, and that's not a commitment. Commitment is not an opinion; commitment is a fact. If you are true, you're true; and if you're wrong, you're wrong. Commitment to your family means at all costs you make time and make sure that you say and do what you think is best even though weeks later you might see that you were wrong but you stood for what you believed in. Your commitment is being able to apologize for what you've done and be happy that you had growth to see that you were wrong and you were able to admit it.

Husband, wife…commitment is vows of "I do" that means forever. Before you walk down the aisle you have to think of it truly — Can I be? Can I do? Can I live with you for the rest of my life? If you can it's a huge commitment but simple. Obey and listen; be partners and be a team. No one is superior over the other. Your voices are the same if you speak at once. When you speak individually somehow it makes you stand for different reasons, so think about whom you are marrying and why you are marrying. The commitment is forever.

Girlfriend, boyfriend; it's a commitment that means we as two are in a situation where we are thinking about being as one. Taking the steps to understand one another, learning their laughter, the dos, the don'ts, and being able to mesh together and find the greatest reasons why we love each other at our worst moments. That's what commitment is all about. Commitment is being true to not just you but to the ones that you stand in front of. That's what commitment is all about.

Walking down the street the ones that you love so much are nowhere around. When you see that reflection of your shadow following you it should remind you of the commitment that you have. You are not alone. Someone loves you the way that you love them. It's very important what you say and what you do because it doesn't just affect you. When it affects your sisters, your brothers, or your significant other that decision has to be thought of because it's true love that is in the balance of the decisions that you make.

Humble the heart that you have, accept your love, and be graceful. Keep the spirit within you and always search for the goodness in everything. When a decision needs to be made, don't be selfish. Think of others and think of you. Put it together and you'll see what you are supposed to do.

Commitment.

By K. Owens

This page is for You

Your chance to write about your friend or someone you love or just about yourself in your own words.

So now you are a part of this book.

A Million

Have you ever thought about how much a million is?
A million could be so much if you look at the small picture one by one.
Are you willing to look at the small picture?
The small picture is a million hugs can change your life and others.
A million ways to say I love you.
We are all capable to give a million plus.
So let's start giving it.

When I say million, is money the first thing that comes to mind?
Put money out of your mind and there will be a million things in your heart to find.
The perfect love story can start off by saying I'll give you a million. I'll give you a million ways to find love within us. I give you a million reasons to want to stay. I give you a million reasons to want to do things right in your life. Do you think you're capable of holding someone's hand a million times? Because you can hold it in your mind when you're thinking of them. You can dream of holding and unfolding your arms to give hugs to show love. Picking up the phone once with the intentions of calling again. There's a start. Saying I'm sorry and knowing that you'll never make the same mistake again intentionally.

There's a start...

Counting your blessings is the perfect start.

How many steps have you taken up to this point?

How many breaths have you taken?

How many heartbeats have you felt and how many have you felt of others?

Can you feel the passion of life within your fingertips?

Do you remember everything that you've done over the last week? And if you don't I'm quite sure we all know someone who does. Being thankful for who you are and where you are. Knowing that there's no way that we can keep count of all the blessings that we received throughout the years but somehow we always manage to keep count of all the bad things. When someone walks up to you and asks you what do you have why do we pause and have to think about it?

When someone asks you the same question about what you don't? It's the easiest question to answer.

A million can be the worst thing that ever happens to you, if you look at it in a material sense. A million is the best thing in your life when you think about happiness, family, friends, love, and counting the minutes that you have with one another. And what we're doing to change each other with unselfish intentions. A million ways to smile. Let's make a million reasons to show that we are worthy to have seconds, minutes, hours, days, months, and years. Coming together as one overcoming our fears. That's real. Think about it — we should be grateful where there's no minute wasted. Have you ever thought about how many people's lives had to change and had to make change so we can see change? How many people have died before us?? Millions!

How many lives are you going to change?
So they can see change to have change in their lives...
Someone has died for us, someone has cried for us and carried a cross for us.

Now it's our turn..
What are we going to do?
Now somehow a million does not seem out of reach...it's simple.

Live your life giving, hugging, kissing, holding hands, and being true friends. When you give a million, it's not because you want it in return; it's because you're living your millions breathing, understanding, and possessing your soul.
Being grateful for the past and willing to give millions for the days to come.
Now that's love.

No money, no materials can measure up just sitting next to someone eating a bowl of cereal; now that's love.

By
K. Owens

Finding Your Happy

Finding what makes you happy.

You should not find what makes you happy because you should be happy for the fact that you are here.

It's so weird that being happy has been so twisted over the years.

Most people think in order to be happy you have to have something or somebody.

So when you're broke and you walk around with your head down, does that mean that someone has to put something in your pocket in order for you to be happy?

And if that's the case, every dime and every nickel that you spend, your smile turns into a grin.

That's not the way it's supposed to be.

Life has many ups and downs.

If you can find you're happy in the moments when you are on your last leg and still have the will to smile and laugh from your heart and your soul and just be able to embrace the moment that you are going through, and being happy that you'll see through because your heart and your spirit is real.

It possesses you, and that's what gives you the smile on your face because you know there will be another sunny day.

Let's not let cars, money, and clothes, people...change us to make us happy.

Let's be happy on our own.

So when we have those things we are still the same person and we walk the same, nothing's changed just because we have a little pocket change.

New car, clothes...have the spirit in your heart, put the joy through your walk, walk with pride.

Even if you have tears in your eyes...it's okay.

Tears are for growth.

It makes you grow because when you can feel sorrow for something when your heart bleeds to the point where you cry, it makes you stronger for the next time, the next day, the next situation.

You have to unload the weight that you have.

That's why you have to believe.

As long as you believe, you will achieve.

I found myself sitting across the table from someone and I asked him..."What is wrong? How come you have your head down today? Why are you so sad?"

His first words were — "All my bills are due, my mom is arguing at me, everybody needs this, and everybody needs that. What am I to do? What is there for me to be happy about?"

And I said to him, "Just look at my eyes. Look deep in my eyes and if you can really see the reflection of yourself...that's what you should be happy about."

Be happy because you can see it and you're sitting to see it.

So the control is yours.

I'm not saying be happy all the time walking around with a big Kool-aid smile on your face. I'm saying within your heart have the amazing grace.

So you're graceful and you're grateful for what you do have.

So when the moment comes when you have more than what you have now, life is still great.

Where you're headed and your goals, nothing's changed.

Just because it's raining outside and you don't have an umbrella doesn't mean that you need to wait.

And if it's hot and you don't have a fan to cool you down, that doesn't mean that it's the end of the world. You can find shade.

So you can find it no matter what.

There's always an answer.

Just don't go off your first response, because your first response is usually a quick decision.

If you think about it you can think more logically about what needs to be done.

So let's slow down and just feel because you are in control of your life.

Each step that you take is for your fate and what changes your life throughout the day.

So pay attention to what you have inside.

Oh it's so wonderful when the tables are turned.

When all the bad times become good times.

The times when you were down, you're standing.

When you had not, now you have.

Those are great moments.

Appreciate it for what it is, but appreciate who you are more when you didn't have it so you can still be you when you do have it.

Finding your happy...find what makes YOU happy. Search.

And when I say search I'm not saying walk outside. Go look around the room, find the nearest mirror or close your eyes and then you can see it clear because it's you. You make you happy.

Have you ever told a joke and you laugh before you got it out? Because you talk to yourself before it even came out. That's your happy.

Have you been driving down the street and started smiling for no reason?

There's your happy.

Listening to music, dancing...there's your happy.

So when the music is turned off you might not dance but keep the romance that you have for yourself in being yourself. You don't need anything else for you to be you. Just strive to be the best and have the best in your life. Don't change; just rearrange the things in your life that fit for you.

There's your happy. Think about someone in your life that means so much to you.

Really think about it. Who is it and why do they take that part of your heart to make you happy?

Think about the people that you make happy. Oh we can all be sad at one time, but it's so wonderful when we are all happy at the same time. Each person might have or have not. Some might have a little more than the others but it does not matter, because we can't take it with us. What we can take with us is that joyful heart and soul that you laugh with. Fill it up as much as you can. Overflow so it runs down your body. Let it overflow. Finding your happy...find it within yourself and you will be it. Feel it, embrace it, taste it.

That's you, that's real love, and that's your happy, because your happiness is within you.

By
K. Owens

First or Last

It doesn't matter whether I'm first or last.
When I'm standing in line
I'm always first to the one standing behind.
If I have to be last standing in front of heaven's gate,
truly it has been worth the wait.
If you see me standing and humming
with a smile on my face,
I'm just humming the Amazing Grace.

By

K. Owens

Best of Friends

Best of friends — Is that what you are to me?
We talk about everything; we laugh about everything
and cry about all of the above.
I am moody and I have my moments
and you are moody at the same time.
Best friend — Is that what you are to me?
I know you are my best friend because I can tell you anything
and even if you don't understand you still stand by my side.
That does not mean you don't give me a hard time about it,
because you and I both know you do. And only you can do that.
My best friend that is what you are to me.
I sleep a little more at ease.
I am working on my thoughts
so I can be a better person and a better friend.
I wish…you wished…we wished — that we can figure this out.
Less tears and enjoy the years and face all of our fears.
That is what I wish.
My best friend, you're crazy and you know it. I am crazy and I show it!!
We laugh when there is nothing funny just because we are who we are.
Weeks can pass by without a phone call and there is never a moment
missed. Just the thought of you makes me smirk, because I know you
are giving someone a hard time at all times
and you would say the same for me (smiling inside).
Best of friends — how many people can say that and mean it?
Give tough love and grow from it.
Being mad and happy at the same time because you are mad at the
problem that we are facing but happy
that we have each other to get through it.
That is real.
I wouldn't trade you for a million because you have given me trillions.

Best of Friends.

By,
K. Owens

Do You Picture Me?

Can you picture me kissing someone else?

Can you picture me holding their hand
and being happy as can be?

If you can't, that means you're the one in the picture.

The picture is within you
because a picture can't see its own reflection.

By
Kelly Owens

Don't Forget

Don't forget that life is more precious that your eyes can see.

Do you know who you are?

If you don't here's a little hint.

Notice the way you walk. The way your arms

and hands sway in the wind.

Are you true to yourself?

Can you say that you are your friend?

Are you honest with yourself?

Do you believe that you're headed in the right direction?

For instance, when you get finished reading this

where are you headed and why?

Do you believe your purpose in life?

Is it about you? Or the world around you?

Don't forget your heart beats so many times in one minute.

Don't forget who sent you here and why.

And if you don't know here's a clue...

When you get finished reading this look outside, look up and down.

Look all around; look at the trees,

the dirt, the clouds, or even the sun.

Can you feel the wind up against your face?

If you can't feel it you're not standing still long enough,

because the wind always blows.

Can't you feel it coming out your nose?

Your chest never rests; your blood and your veins flow still

while you are able to breathe through your nose.

Your skin covers your whole body

as if it's protecting you from something.

To me, I see your skin around you being the palm of God.

Don't forget who you are.

Can you believe that you still have a chance

to make things right for the things in life that you've done wrong?

Because as long as you can see and be able to read this

you still have a chance to find your purpose in life.

The next time you see and hear anything you should bow to your

knees and pray for the angels to sing.

You have what it takes to change the world.

It starts with you.

So your life is in your hands.

Reach out for it and if you fall,

don't feel bad, because in order to stand one day you have to crawl.

By
K. Owens

Guiding Light

Dark and cloudy day.

Only through You I can see the sunshine,

and on a cold and winter day I feel warm inside.

When the sun is bright as it can be,

I feel Your shade protecting me.

When I'm down on my luck

You inspire me to never give up.

I can feel Your presence surrounding me.

Thank You for taking your time creating me.

By
K. Owens

Your Past and Your Future

Your past is your past. It can't be changed! It's up to you to rearrange your life to make a change. Not saying that your past is bad. Your past is just a life that is passed. So it has nothing to do with the future when it comes to the past, but your past creates your future.

So let's take it as if we want to change our lives to become a better person...to see things differently. Being healthier in what we speak of. Being more content with our life. So let's walk. Let's walk down the path of our past to get to our future.

It's like passing all those trees and those leaves and those things that you used to do and now all of a sudden your vision is changing. Now it's what you're about to do. It's like walking down to a dock and seeing a boat. A little boat with paddles...jumping in just you and your friend and that's you and you past. Paddling for a better future or a better you. The best way to look at your past is to be able to paddle to a bigger boat, a bigger life. I'm not saying forget your past. I'm saying carry a rope so you always can be reminded of your past. So when you get to the bigger boat...don't just get out and let your past float away because you forget about those days. You don't want to forget. You always want to know so you don't make the same mistakes twice.

 294

So tie a rope on that boat that you just got out of and tie it to the back of the big boat that you just got into. No matter how that little boat tugs back on that big boat coming through the waves of people reminding you of your past...that big boat keeps going on.

Every now and then there's nothing wrong with glancing back just to see how that little boat is handling through the rain and the people that used to be your friends.

You're a bigger boat now. You don't have to worry about that anymore. What they say has nothing to do with your day. No matter what kind of waves, it has nothing to do with what you crave. You're for change. You're in a big boat now...a little wave cannot move.

It takes millions of them to move that boat.

So look to your future. Ride it and be strong. Don't let it change you. Your life is in your hands. It's up to you to make it, but you can't do it alone. The big boat that you're on represents your love and your heavenly sent spirit. Pray to keep the big mass around you...to keep you humble upon such rocky waters. And the more you pray the further that rope will be holding the little boat that's trailing your path. Before you know it you won't be able to see it anymore, and that's a good thing because you won't even be able to feel it anymore. That's when you know the boat that you have traveled on anoints you.

So let your past be your past. Let's strive for a better future. Find it in every way that you can. Don't be afraid to ask questions. Don't be afraid to say I'm sorry, and most of all don't be afraid to pray and ask for forgiveness. Your spirit is what helps you glide across the waters. Your soul is the size of the boat that you are traveling on. Wouldn't it be wonderful to name the boat "Being born again"? Now you're riding on the ship that's called "Born Again." And you can gently walk to the back of that ship. You can untie that rope because you've been forgiven for your sins. As long as your boat is a ship, there's always room for others.

So be the greatest captain that there ever was and tell a friend.

Just let them know, it's time to get on board.

By

K. Owens

Your True Friends

People who believed in me because of who I am and what I brought to the table have always surrounded me. I didn't have much, but I had a personality and a drive to do for others and in the same process forgot to do what's right for me.

I found that when I had fallen in a hole I had to stretch up to reach very far for the rope that someone had to pull me out. By the time I got on my tiptoes reaching as far as my body could reach and grabbed that rope to pull myself to the top, I realized that it was the same rope that I tied to the tree before I fell.

There are times when I fell and someone did throw me a rope, and before I could get on my feet again, they had their hand in my pocket. I'm just a little confused about who my true friends are. I'm very happy to know the ones that I can believe in.

True Friends.

By,
K. Owens

Gossip

He said, she said.
Once you say, then you said it.
But is it the truth?
And if it is the truth, how do you know it?
Did you see it?
We've seen many things that we thought were the truth and
realized that they weren't.
So was it?
A man goes into the gym wearing a pair of jeans,
and people are talking about him as if that's so wrong.
But what they didn't realize,
he probably got up late this morning
from being up all night with his kids
from being sick and forgot his workout pants.
But he's so driven for change; he went to the gym anyway.
And we are sitting over in the corner with something to say.
Who is right?
Who is wrong?
I guess nobody knows.
Whose goals are more important
when the people who are gossiping,
wouldn't have come to the gym
if they had forgotten their gym clothes?
He made it anyway and didn't care what anyone had to say.
I guess his goals are different than ours.

We all have pain in our lives at some point in time.
At this moment when you are reading this,
somebody is crying, somebody is dying.

Somebody is in the hospital fighting for their life.
There's been an accident since you've been reading this page.
There's a child missing. There's someone who has passed on.
It's too late for theirs to be changed.
So what are we talking about
when there is so much pain in this world?
In order to get through the pain, we have to make a change.
You, I, we are not perfect.
We've all made mistakes.

I was eating a bowl of cereal while writing this
and started crying for no reason and I don't know why.
I got a phone call and they had an attitude
because they thought I had an attitude.
I was just trying to find out why.
I wasn't in a laughing mood at the time.
But I hope they don't talk about me
and treat me different tomorrow
because I was just trying to drown out my sorrows.
But I love them anyway.
That's what we're supposed to do.
We are all supposed to be headed to heaven
so it doesn't matter who did this, who did that —
because we never really know the true story,
because we are so busy worrying about someone else's story.

So what is our story?
We always have the right way to do it but for some reason,
we always get it wrong sometimes.
And sometimes we think we are right all the time,
when other people think we are wrong.

So are they right or how are we wrong?
I guess that too no one will ever know.
So gossip only hurts people's feelings.
Relationships, lives have changed
just because of something that someone has said
who has been misled.
Now it's what you said when someone told you
and you believed it.

Let's change life.
Look at the positive. There's too much hurt
and pain in this world to talk it.
Let's walk our path and help those who are within our path.
If you see someone down, pray for them.
If you see someone smiling, pray for them too,
because a lot of times we all smile
when we have so much to hide
when we fight the tears in our eyes.
So it's not perfect.
I guess I say that we should say
the only things that happen through our day...
and that's life.
So let's forgive and be forgiven and start all over so we can do
this again.
Let's pray and come to Christ
so we can be born again and be forgiven for our sins.
No more gossip.

By
K. Owens

Friendship and Fatherhood

Friendship to me is forever, and even then it starts all over again. Most people go through life and have no idea of the lives that they are changing. I just want to open your eyes so you can see what I see. Friendship is the word spoken amongst others when your friend is not there and that tells you what kind of friend you are and the way that you think of them. You are a friend to me, a true friend that is. I love the way you spend quality time with your kids. Your family is first. I can hear it in your voice every time that we talk because that love is embedded in your soul. I admire that in you.

I have something that I want to give to you, and it means the world to me because of the frame of mind that I was in when I bought it. It was the first day that I realized that I am somebody and I can be somebody to someone else. This gift I wouldn't give to my own brother, so it is a special gift to you even though my brother means the world to me because I am all about family.

Jonathan, don't ever change your passion for life, your commitment to your wife and your kids, and your drive for success. Working out at 5:00 in the morning as a team, now that is love. Spending time with your wife before it is time to go to work to help continue life and keep a roof over your head. I admire that in you more than you know.

I remember when I was a kid tag was my favorite game to play because I was so good at it. I never realized how important those moments were playing tag with all my friends. I miss them even to this day, and when I think about the challenges of life sometimes my heart gets heavy. I think back to those days where we played like there was no tomorrow. You remind me of the friends I had. I would love to play a game with you. I am looking for a good man and the best father, husband, and neighbor all rolled up in one, so TAG YOU'RE IT!

Now I don't have to turn back the hands of time to find friendship. Now I look forward to the present time because I have a friend. What do you give a man who has everything? You give him something sentimental. One day I will tell you the story about where my frame of mind was when this watch was purchased and why. It couldn't have been given to a better father and friend.

Friendship and Fatherhood.

By,
K. Owens

Why?

Why do people argue? It's either you said that or you did this or no, you said that or you did that. One way or another, it doesn't matter, because something is wrong. To understand, it's not to look at what was wrong; it's to look at the way to make it right. To understand that we all are not perfect; we do make mistakes. Just because we do make a mistake it doesn't mean that we don't love you. It doesn't mean that we had intentions of disrespecting you. Most mistakes are made unintentionally. Just off the cuff. It's so simple. Someone asks you a question and you answer it. Five minutes later, you wish you'd answered it differently. Nothing's wrong; just make it right. Standing up for what you believe in, no matter what it is.

Look within yourself and see what it is that you're fighting for before you speak of it. If you don't, you are speaking and not knowing where you're headed. So face it first, understand what you've done wrong and why. Sometimes why you did it wrong, there's no answer because sometimes we never know. The fact is, if you know that you're better than a decision that you've made, you have room to make it right.

So what you have to do is...two people. Look to see why you love or have fallen in love, and there's your answer. The answer to all of your problems is in the beginning of your relationship or the beginning of the "Hi, how are you doing? What's your name?" You are blessed. You want to be someone that the other person could be interested in. So think back to why you fell in love at the peak of being angry. Let's not let the mistakes in our lives change our lives. Let's allow the change that we make in our lives change our lives for a better future.

Look into each other's eyes when you are at the peak of being upset and step back and just relax and realize there was always a beginning. If you live your life the same way you lived the beginning, you will always have a wonderful ending. Believe in each other. Listen to one another. LISTEN TO ONE ANOTHER. Even if you don't understand. Sometimes it's not for you to understand, but the fact that you're listening to understand is enough. Stand by each other on the decisions that you make, because your dreams and her dreams or his dreams can be different than your dreams, but your dream together is still a dream.

So calm down, relax, and remember where your relationship began.

Let's not argue. Keep it real.

By
Kelly Owens

Trying to be Hard

Trying to be hard wearing your suit, with an attitude.
Walking down the street as if you are the best thing
that the world has ever made.
Driving your Escalade with a chip on your shoulder.
Or saggy pants down to your knees.
Sitting in a room with your friends smoking weed.
Trying to be hard.
Just having an attitude for no reason.
Cutting somebody off, driving crazy.
Always had something to say about somebody...
as if we can do it better.
Trying to be hard.

The hardest thing about being hard is you lose yourself,
because you are behind the image,
so you can never see who you truly are.
So you being hard shouldn't matter what you drive,
what you smoke or where you are at...
or the chip that you have on your shoulder...
or the fact that you are older than the person that is next to you.
It shouldn't matter when it comes to respect.

Let me tell you what's hard that should be easy if you want to be hard.
Let someone cut you off and give you the finger.
Try to be hard and smile.
Let someone do you wrong and you say... that's okay.
Try to be hard.
Go to Bible study in the middle of a week,
after you've worked all day or sat around all day.

Let's try to be hard.
Let's try to face the hardest things in life because life is hard on
its own.
We don't have to be hard when it comes to anything.
We just have to be stronger to get through the hard times.
When you are hard and life is already hard,
then you have an attitude and you are rude...
with a chip on your shoulder.
There's no gain in that.
Usually you are alone and you are getting more upset
because you are creating all the negativity that comes to you.
So you get treated rude and people treat you different
but you don't realize that it's because of the energy that you are
putting out.
If you walk in the store and your jeans are down to your feet,
or to the bottom of your butt...
Good luck trying to be respected as if you are going to buy
something.
I'm not saying that it's wrong to wear your pants that way; that's
you.
Don't try to be hard just being you.

You can be you with a smile on your face.
You can be you and go to church on Sunday.
You can be you.
When hard times come to you instead of being hard to someone
else,
try to be hard and work them through it
to find the sensitive side so you can see through it.
So focus.
It's within you.
Christ has given us all an inner joy, an inner love, an inner spirit...
and a soul that you can live on.

So breathe through it, walk through it, the passion of life is yours
—

you just have to humble yourself to be able to see it.
So it's not all about being gangsta or being hard
or thinking that you are better because you make more money,
or drive a better this or have nicer that.
Those things don't matter.
The only thing that matters is you are being you.
So take it what it is...
Drive up to someone who is catching the bus,
and smile at them, don't look down on them.
You could be riding a bike and someone is riding a skateboard...
you are equal.

The kid on the skateboard is equal
to the man that is flying that jet plane.
Because in Christ's eyes, we all are the same.
He doesn't have an attitude to us...
because we've accomplished this or we accomplished that.
He blesses us for the trials and tribulations that we get through
and stand up and face it and take a step —
so He can take a step to show us life so we can have life.

So the fight is not with the people you see.
The fight is with the entities of life
that make life so hard in the first place.
So let's not be hard and if we are going to be hard,
let's be hard about making things right in our life
and accepting Christ in our life...
then it's not hard at all, it's just ups and downs.

By,
K. Owens

True Friend

Where are our true friends?
If I fall today, will my friends come today or tomorrow?
If I'm in need, will they be the first to come and plant that seed,
for me to grow?

When I'm cold and I'm alone, will they talk to me and comfort
me,
when I call them on the phone?
Will they be too busy to listen to my pain?
Will someone run to help me...
when they can't run on their own?
Will someone call me...

When they don't have a phone and they have to use someone
else's?
Will they make the effort to go above and beyond...
just to show that real love?
Will they be the way that I am with them?

When you give your heart to help people get through the dark,
it's nice when you receive it on the other end from a true friend.
Will my friends give me excuses?
Or will the excuse be the excuse that they have to give to their
job,
to get off to make sure that I'm okay?
What will it be?

Because I'm trying to find a friend today.
For my friends that I've helped and been there when they were in
need,
will they do it just because I've done it for them?

Will they do it just because they are my friend and it's not payback?
They do it because our friendship is all that.
What would it be?

Will my friends treat me different when they get their tax returns?

A true friend is a friend that is a friend to the end.
No matter what we get through it together.
No matter what the weather, we weather the storm.
No matter whose arm, we pull together so it's OUR strength.
That's a true friend...

A true friend is someone who never forgets what has been done for them.
Even the little things, because most people forget.
Most people when you call them to ask them to be there for you,
they forgot all the times that you've been there for them.
I don't know if you want someone to be there for you
just because you've been there for them.
You want it to be because they're your friend...
because there is no scorecard.
The sad thing about it is-

It hurts more when you know that you are giving love to show love,
and when you ask for it in return, there are always excuses.

I'm trying to find a true friend.
I have some true friends and I'm thankful for that.
So few and far between but I do have some.
The ones that I thought were true friends, I found out that they weren't.

Because when their problems came to an end,
I was the last one that they called a friend.
The ones that have and have not
they still love me just as well as the sun is shining...
that is a true friend.

That is a friend not just because they are on the receiving end.
The ones on the receiving end are the first to give you excuses...
Not today, not tomorrow, maybe next week.
So find your true friend and your true friends
and first of all find the friend within you...
and then you can see the friend within them.

By
K. Owens

Sweet Distraction

It's so sweet to be distracted by someone with such depth.
My decision is indecisive.
I don't know whether to walk up
and say hi or just let you be.
I felt something about you
that is such a sweet distraction to me.
I believe in faith.
I dropped what I was doing just to say hi.
I could tell that you had a lot on your mind,
so I just smiled to give you hope
and to show you some sunshine from within,
because I too was trying to say hi to someone
that can be a friend.
So here we go, here is a shirt that says *One Love*
that represents strength, love and unity.
Thanks for the dance, and here are some flowers
so you can continue your smile,
and all you have to do is give them some sunshine,
so they can last for a while.
Thanks for being understanding and free with me.
Thanks for the dance with a little touch of romance.
We can make a fruit salad and just watch a movie.
You can take my hand and spin me around.
You can dance like there's air beneath your feet.
So I trust in and believe in faith
so you can call me Froggy cause I'm about leap.

By
K. Owens

My Celebrities

When I was young, my celebrities were the people I grew up around.
The people I looked up to:
my grandma, my grandpa, my mom, my uncle, my aunties...
those were my celebrities.
I didn't care about what I saw on TV, because TV wasn't reality to me.
When I saw my celebrities those were the ones that I wanted to follow.
I could see an aunt that cooks a cake like no other
and the taste it just melts in your mouth.
And I have an aunt who can sew a shirt like a shirt has never been made before.
I have an uncle who knew everything about every car that had ever been driven.
And if I ever wanted to throw a football or play sports, I know an uncle
that knows every move that had ever been made as if he'd made them himself.
So my celebrities were within my family...
my uncles and aunties and my grandma and my grandpa and my mom.
Those are the celebrities to me.
When I see something great I see it in their eyes.
When I see someone facing life and making choices I see it in their faith.
I see it in their FAITH. Those are my celebrities.
I go to church with my grandpa...
catching the bus to go to different churches throughout the valley.
I come home, my grandma was humming in the kitchen while she's cooking...

pancakes, biscuits, whatever it is it was the best smell that we smelled
when we were growing up as kids.
My mom always told us what was right and what was wrong
and she gave us the reason to want to live on.
My uncles and my aunties they always had something that was dear to me.
I've always wanted to follow or chase but when I had seen their face,
I was happy about my race.
I had no doubt about life when I was surrounded by nothing but love
because that's all I seen was love.
Everyday there was a phone call to our home and it was for someone.
Every day I had seen a phone call going out from my mom to someone else.
I hear about all the things that she talked about on the phone
and that's why I live my life through my celebrities because I don't care about TV.
So I'm thankful to be a part of this family and this special tree.
If I had to come up with a fruit that would be on this tree it would be...
Apples, Bananas, Peaches, Mangos.
It would be every fruit that there is,
because that's what I got from my family since we were kids.
So I love them because when I look up all I see is my family tree.
When I look in the mirror all I see is me.
So the ingredients in the water or whatever it took for that tree to grow...
when I look in the mirror it definitely shows.
I am thankful to Christ for the tree that grows within me.

By
K. Owens

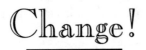

Change!

Write down some of the changes you're going to make in your life

Merry Christmas

We've all seen the same things on the way home...the sign that says Lucas Lane... or your own sign that greets you as you enter your neighborhood.

We sit inside our homes and watch the kids ride their bikes and four-wheelers without a care in the world.

This truly is a gift.

Each home you see wrapped in bricks or stucco is the wrapping paper of our homes.

Can you see the gifts? This Christmas is special to us all!

We've learned so much about each other and so little at times, which keeps us close.

It's another year's end, and we leave the past behind. We live every day as if there is no yesterday, but we take our blessings from yesterday to help us conquer tomorrow.

So this Christmas season the gift is when you wake up and look into the mirror and know He's already given it. Let's show the world a neighborhood's love that's worth writing about and a legacy to be published.

K. Owens

My Angel

Thanks for taking the time to see what I see: Here is an angel that I found sitting on the side of the road, and I spotted it from a mile away; and what is so special about it is that I didn't see it with my eyes. I felt it with my spirit. And I felt tears falling down my face the closer I got to it. And when I picked it up, my hand was full of the tears of wondering why I asked God to send me a blessing and he sent me an angel, and the closer I put this ball to my face I started humming Amazing Grace and I started to squint to see it more clearly and I saw the face that resembled yours. They say a crystal ball can show you the future, but I say a crystal ball with an angel inside is your future. And you just have to realize that life is in the palm of your hands. So thanks for being the angel that I don't have to open my eyes to see. Thanks for being an angel and being a part of me.

Reality... I took my hands to wipe the tears from my eyes and I saw what I never thought I would have; it was my reflection of my own eye in the mirror, and the water below is me trying to hold back the tears so I can see a little clearer. And the angel inside was a heaven-sent gift. And the angel that had your face that had me humming Amazing Grace represents how I see you.

Your friend forever on earth and beyond.

By K. Owens

Sorry

I'm sorry for making the wrong decision when I knew it was
wrong from the start.
I'm sorry for not listening
when I knew you were right.
I'm sorry for being right
when I knew I was wrong.
I'm sorry for the days when I knew I should have called you on
the phone and I didn't.
I'm sorry for smiling in your face
when I knew I had so much to hide.
I'm sorry for being young
and not knowing what the future holds.
I'm sorry for all the little things you were told.
I'm sorry for being me,
when I didn't know who me was.
I'm sorry for chasing love just
for the sake of because.
I'm sorry for the changes that I had to go through in life to find
me.
I'm sorry for acting like I didn't care.
I'm sorry I didn't know
how to care or how to love.
I always knew what the word love, forever, together, honest,
wholeheartedly, and being true sounded like.
I just didn't know what the words mean.
I didn't know what it felt like until...
I

Lost

You.

By K. Owens

The Key to Life

The key to life is for all of us to find whatever it is that brings happiness within our hearts. As long as we are happy, we do good things and we make good choices. We are all faced with challenges that make us face ourselves and find a part of us that we don't want to face. We have to face it in order to go on. It can be something or someone but we have to find that challenge because we have to be someone. That's why they are called the challenges of life.

Sickness, health, betrayal, broken hearts.
Flat tires, unpaid bills, and the job that you don't want to be at.
Friends you know that aren't true friends, lies, all of the above.

When in some way, shape, or form we all are searching for true love, true happiness, and laughter — the greatest gifts. The greatest friends...friends that are friends when other friends are not there and they are still friends. A job that we want to go to even when we are sick because it is a part of us. A family that we are proud of even when we are hurting at times. That's what it's all about.

This life is not perfect for you or me. We always find reasons to want to cry and find silent moments riding in the car with no music or listening to something that we never listen to and realize that we are lost within the moments when we are just trying to find the right way to find life.

Finding that true friend — someone who is honest and true. Even though you can battle from time to time, it's real because it is real.

Only fakeness becomes hate. When you have hate in your heart it blinds you from all the true love and the good things that life has to offer. You only see the negative things that are in life. Trying to find the positive things are the hardest to find when you are blindfolded. True friends help you see through it because when you don't have eyes to see they are the ones that let you know what you should see and how it should be. Even though you have to make your own decision it's best to have someone who has been positive to give you a reason to want to live.

That's the key to life.

By K. Owens

What is it Going to Take?

What is it going to take for us to be able to read something and actually apply it into our lives today? We can read titles, whether you choose a Never-ending story, Peaceful sleep, I apologize, Can you imagine, Little Lady, I wonder, What if? Yes, I wonder what if? What if and why are we slowing down when we should be speeding up? What is it going to take for us to read things on the page and actually apply it in our lives today?

When you read something and it sounds good and it feels good, does it move you? If it does move you, are you going to do something about it? The change is not because of the change, because it's written about change. The change is for us to get up on our feet to make a change...so let's make a change. Let's read something that's meaningful. Let's start worrying about the things that we need to change, and it can start right now.

Not today, RIGHT NOW.

Tomorrow can be the best step that you've ever taken, because today was the decision that you made it. Let's read things that uplift our heart and that seed that was planted within us. Let's feel it from our heart. Let's make it happen. Reading something and it says — don't forget. Don't forget about your life and how you got here.

Then how do we? How do we get through this? Me and you. There's no me without you. Alcohol. Alcohol is a reality that is not a reality. Then first and last. It doesn't matter whether I'm first and last. Single mothers — it's about a child growing up in a home with one parent. So that can be applied to fathers.

Today is a good day. Smile from your heart and from your soul. Sunshine, moon, and your smile...it's about glancing over and seeing sunlight within someone's spirit. Wants and needs are views about what we want in our life and what we need in our life and our desires and passion to figure out which is more important. Our secret...our secret is not having a secret. It's about following your heart, about what is to be and what is not to be. Our past...our past is always something that we've been afraid of at times but we just ask for forgiveness.

Facing the world...facing the world is waking up feeling that you can conquer it and actually reaching for it. Yesterday and today...those are the days that we have, and we're praying for our tomorrows. I am, you are, we are, us...we can be that umbrella to protect someone in the rain.

Guiding light...it's a dark and cloudy day, and only through you we can see sunshine. Born again...live your life as if there is no yesterday. College...is for knowledge. Your blessings are everything that you are feeling right now and your presence in the space that you feel. That's real.

Sweet distraction...sweet distraction is something that is sweet to you and it distracts you at the same time. Our Moms Raised Us Better than this...yes they did raise us better than this. Lost and Found...we all get lost but we can be found. Love and Anger...is conquer an anger at the peak of being misunderstood and have the will to listen. Dream...we all would like to live that dream and have that dream.

A cup of coffee...you can throw it on me. You are not responsible for the first response. Filter...filter the things through your mind, that goes to your heart so by the time it gets to your soul it's something that moves you.

Do you picture me...picturing someone that you love with someone else knowing that the someone else is you. Can you picture that? Why...why is life this way? I wish...I wished for many things. We wish for many things. What is it going to take for us to get them?

All these words and all these poems that can be written...they can be so moving but they don't move anything if you don't get up and move. You've got to use the tools that you have to grasp life, to go out there and get it. To get up and stop talking about it. We have to reach out for our dreams and start living it. Dreams are a wonderful thing if it's reality.

Tomorrow always can be a better day. Headed to heaven on the airline...you can buy your ticket, start right now. Asking for some forgiveness and the goodness of the steps that you take are preserving your fate for that ticket. So it doesn't matter what plane you board.

Come walk with me...come walk with Christ. Let's walk the ground the same way that he walked it. We can't bear the pain that he did, but we can walk the same that he did because we are his children. I believe in my blessings...do you believe in your blessings? You should — your reading, your sitting, standing, and breathing. There's a blessing to be heard. Speak out and tell somebody what your blessing is.

Can you imagine...after all of this we look back to someone that gave so much just to have the moment that we have now? Let's take these seconds, minutes, hours, days, months, years. Let's drown out the tears and find happiness within them. Let's find Christ within ourselves, and let's live for ourselves and others. Because life is not just about us; it's about what we find in us to change others while we are changing ourselves. So when you leave this world, make sure you leave it the best way.

Celebrities...your celebrities can be anyone who is dear to you that you look up to. You don't necessarily have to follow in their footsteps, because that's their life. That's the way that they do it. That's the way that he or she said it. Your voice is so different. That is your voice. Speak your voice and let it be heard. And if you are not confident about what you have to say, hold it until the right day comes along. Be it before you see it. Achieve it, then show it to the world.

A never-ending story...that's what it's all about. It's about all of our dreams. All of our steps and everything that we've ever been through. Our ups and downs, our tears, our fears. Love, hate, anger, conquering it all. Writing from our blood because when we hurt we feel it deep, and when you love, love deep, but let that love come to the surface. Because love is not love if you can't show it. It could be inner love. That is great. But the real love is that inner love that you want to show and share with the world.

So let's read something that is passionate to us. Something uplifting to give us such an overcoming experience like the Holy Ghost. Find it. Just look within the mirror and you'll see yourself. Just the way your body works with itself. Getting yourself dressed and your hands and gripping whatever it is that it's gripping.

The way they work together is the way we should all work together. Let's not lose our dreams. Let's make our dream; because our dream is not someone else's dream doesn't mean that it's not a dream. It's OUR dreams. There are millions and millions and millions of dreams. Let's let it be a waterfall that leads down to a perfect stream.

Can you see your face in the reflection of that stream?

Can you feel that Holy Ghost?

Can you feel the spirit within you?

Can you feel it? Can you imagine?

Can you imagine a waterfall of all of our dreams

leading down to a perfect stream?

CAN YOU IMAGINE?

By

K. Owens